FIGHTING TECHNIQUES OF THE ELITE FORCES

How to Train and Fight like the Special Operations Forces of the World

LEROY THOMPSON

Skyhorse Publishing

First published in 2005 by Greenhill Books. First paperback edition published in 2015 by Frontline Books, an imprint of Pen & Sword Books Ltd.

Skyhorse Publishing books may be purchased in bulk at special discounts for sales promotion, corporate gifts, fund-raising, or educational purposes. Special editions can also be created to specifications. For details, contact the Special Sales Department, Skyhorse Publishing, 307 West 36th Street, 11th Floor, New York, NY 10018 or info@skyhorsepublishing.com.

Skyhorse® and Skyhorse Publishing® are registered trademarks of Skyhorse Publishing, Inc.®, a Delaware corporation.

Visit our website at www.skyhorsepublishing.com.

10 9 8 7 6 5 4 3 2 1

Library of Congress Cataloging-in-Publication Data is available on file.

Cover design by Tom Lau
Cover photo credit: Getty Images

ISBN: 978-1-5107-5448-5
Ebook ISBN: 978-1-5107-5452-2

Printed in the United States of America

FIGHTING TECHNIQUES OF THE ELITE FORCES

Contents

CONTENTS

Illustrations

Diagrams

Abbreviations

Abn	Airborne
ARG	Amphibious Ready Group
ASDS	Advanced SEAL Delivery System
ASDV	Advanced SEAL Delivery Vehicle
ATAK	Advanced Tactical Assault Knife
BUD/S	Basic Underwater Demolition/SEAL
CCP	Communicator's Checkpoint
CCT	Combat Control Team
CIA	Central Intelligence Agency
COPP	Combined Operations Pilotage Parties
CQB	Close Quarters Battle
CRRC	Compact Rubber Raiding Craft
CSEL	Combat Survivor Evader Locator
DDS	Dry-Deck Shelter
DPV	Desert Patrol Vehicle
DZ	Drop Zone
E&E	Escape and Evasion
FAV	Fast Attack Vehicle
FEST	Field Epidemiological Survey Team
GCMA	Groupement de Commandos Mixtes Aeroportes
GPS	Global Positioning System
HAHO	High-Altitude High Opening
HALO	High-Altitude Low Opening
HAPPS	High-Altitude Parachute-Penetration System
HARP	High-Altitude Release Point
HE	High Explosive
HMMWV	High-Mobility Multi-Purpose Wheeled Vehicle
IBL	Inflatable Boat, Large
IR	Infrared
JOES	Jungle Operations Extraction System
JSOMTC	Joint Special Operations Medical Training Center
KSK	Kommando Spezialkrafte
LMG	Light machine-gun
LOLEX	Low-Level Extraction
LRDG	Long-Range Desert Group

ABBREVIATIONS

LSV	Light Strike Vehicle
LZ	Landing Zone
MACV/SOG	Military Assistance Commando Vietnam/Special Operations Group
MEUSOC	Marine Expeditionary Unit, Special Operations Capable
MFF	Military Free Fall
MNVS	Mini Night Vision Sight
MoD	Ministry of Defence
MSHR	Miniature Secure Handheld Radio
NBC	Nuclear, Biological, and Chemical
NVG	Night Vision Goggles
ODA	Operational Detachment A
OP	Observation Post
OSS	Office of Strategic Services
PBC	Patrol Boat, Coastal
PBL	Patrol Boat, Light
RAID	Reaction, Assistance, Intervention, Dissuasion
RHIB	Rigid-Hull Inflatable Boat
SADM	Special Atomic Demolition Munitions
SAMs	Surface-to-Air Missiles
SAS	Special Air Service
SBS	Special Boat Section
SDV	SEAL Delivery Vehicle
SEAL	Sea, Air, Land
SFAS	Special Forces Assessment and Selection
SFG	Special Forces Group
SFQC	Special Forces Qualification Course
SLCD	Spring-Loaded Camming Device
SMG	Sub-Machine Gun
SNLG	Special Naval Landing Force
SOCOM	Special Operations Commando
SOE	Special Operations Executive
SOFLAM	Special Operations Forces Laser Acquisition Marker
SOPMOD	Special Operations Peculiar Modified Version
SOPs	Standard Operating Procedures
SOV	Special Operations Vehicle
SPIE	Special Procedures Insertion/Extraction
STABO	Stabilised Airborne Body Operations
TA	Territorial Army
TCCC	Tactical Combat Casualty Care
TO&E	Tables of Organisation and Equipment
TOW	Tube-launched, Optically tracked, Wire command link guided missile
TUSK	Tactical Utility Sniper's Knife
UDT	Underwater Demolition Team
UNPIK	United Nations Partisans in Korea
USMC	United States Marine Corps
VBSS	Visit, Board, Search, Seize
WMD	Weapon of Mass Destruction

Preface

Truly to cover all of the skills needed by the special operator would require an entire library of books on a wide array of topics. In fact, many special ops soldiers have an entire bookshelf filled with volumes covering the various training they have received, which they often review prior to a deployment. These books are not intended to stand alone but to be a supplement to hands-on training. Operators may use them to review training they received at some point in the past, but a photograph or diagram showing how to rig a rope bridge is most effective if the operator has actually rigged a bridge and crossed a river using it.

This book is meant to act as an overview of the numerous skills necessary to allow special ops troops to carry out a myriad of missions. However, I did not feel that space allowed me to cover many specialised fighting techniques in detail. The irony of special operations is that the operator may use the most modern technology in performing his mission yet may ride a mule to reach his area of operations or may slit an enemy's throat to maintain operational security. This juxtaposition of the most high-tech with the most primitive military skills is one of the most fascinating aspects of special ops. Though it is beyond the scope of this work to cover tactical details on such missions as PoW rescues, prisoner snatches, counter-terrorist ops, selective degrading of the enemy command structure (e.g., assassination), etc., many aspects of such missions are touched upon.

Nevertheless, this book offers a good introduction to the methods special operations troops use to train for their specialised missions, the insertion techniques for getting them to their areas of operations, the methods they use to operate in hostile environments, and their techniques for gathering tactical and strategic intelligence.

Leroy Thompson

FIGHTING TECHNIQUES OF THE ELITE FORCES

Chapter 1

Origins of Special Operations

As long as there has been warfare there have been certain elite troops who were assigned the most dangerous missions. From the Theban Sacred Band, the Spartans, Alexander's Companions, Persia's Immortals, and Caesar's Xth Legion, elite military formations have existed for thousands of years. However, many of these ancient units were elite shock troops, whereas true special operations troops are small highly trained forces whose task it is to carry out missions to strike surgically at an enemy's command and control, to scout or to disrupt logistics. But there are early examples of special operations: when passing through what is now Afghanistan Alexander recruited mountaineers from among his forces to scale the heights and deny them to the enemy; another early special operation occurred during the Punic Wars, when Roman legionaries were sent to North Africa to raise and train guerrillas to fight against the Carthaginians.

During the Dark and Middle Ages some armies contained troops whose specialised functions approximated to those of modern special operators. The Byzantines, for example, employed small units to raise and advise mercenary forces and to sow discord among enemies. Other medieval armies contained specialists in infiltrating cities during sieges and in gathering intelligence. In fact, for hundreds of years special troops who could hasten the fall of a besieged city through a *coup de main* were highly valued. In at least a few cases, the use of swimmers or personnel in small boats to infiltrate a city's defences foreshadowed today's combat swimmers.

The development of the military rifle encouraged the use of small groups of marksmen for special purposes. Since the rifle did not rely on massed fire, as the musket had, small groups of riflemen could be used as skirmishers or sent to carry out 'special' missions. In some cases, riflemen were used to target officers, with a view to disrupting the enemy's command and control. In the United States, Rogers Rangers formed during the French and Indian Wars became the forerunners of all future American special operations personnel. Used for deep reconnaissance and raiding, their mission remains a primary one for US Army Rangers and other special operations troops.

The title 'Rangers' was also applied during the American Civil War to a Confederate mounted raiding unit, Mosby's Rangers, which carried out many behind-the-lines missions. At least some consideration was given during the nineteenth century to using balloons to place troops behind enemy lines, a forerunner of later airborne and airmobile insertions. Towards the end of the nineteenth century, the Boer Commandos proved highly effective irregular forces and and it was they who added the term 'commando' to the lexicon of special operations. By the late nineteenth century, too, many armies incorporated troops who were designated 'scouts,' *'jäger'* or the equivalent in other languages. Often assigned missions which today would fall to long-range patrol units, these light infantrymen were true forerunners to today's special operations troops.

By World War I, other special missions troops had evolved. The German 'Stormtroopers' who were trained to infiltrate Allied trench lines and create confusion in the rear are often cited among the predecessors of today's special forces, but other World War I examples may be cited as well. T. E. Lawrence's raising of indigenous guerrilla forces against the Turks is a classic 'special forces' mission, while the US advocate of airpower, Billy Mitchell, had plans to train small raiding parties using parachutes late in the war.

Between the two World Wars, special operations development took place in various parts of the world, often to meet local circumstances. The US Marines, for example, made extensive use of small patrols and military advisors during the 'Banana Wars,' employing them in missions similar to those later carried out by the Special Forces. In the Soviet Union, the development of airborne forces was initially predicated upon their use in small raiding parties, while the USMC experiments with small boat operations were also designed to insert raiding parties. By the mid-1930s, Italy was experimenting with 'human torpedoes', forerunners of their combat swimmer units which achieved notable success during World War II. Germany, Japan, and Italy followed the Soviet Union in the development of airborne forces. Initially, too, these were seen as small raiding units, but their missions would change as larger airborne forces were developed. Experiments in the USA, Spain, France, Poland, and Great Britain, among other countries, attempted to formulate tactical doctrine for parachute troops just prior to World War II.

Among the first 'special forces' units formed for World War II service was Germany's 'Brandenburgers', a unit which after its formation in 1939 was used for an array of special missions, including many *coup de main* operations. Later in the war, the *Jagdsverbund* under the command of Otto Skorzeny carried out a variety of special operations, including the rescue of Mussolini. The Italians continued to develop their underwater special operations capability early in World War II and carried out raids against British warships in Alexandria and Gibraltar harbours. It was the British, however, who developed the widest array of special operations troops during World War II, to a large extent because during the early years of the War the only way to take the offensive was by carrying out raids against German occupied areas.

The Commandos were developed specifically as seaborne raiders and named because of Churchill's memories of the Boer Commandos he had encountered in South Africa. The Special Operations Executive (SOE) was also formed primarily to carry out operations against occupied Europe, though operations in the Far and Middle East would come under their purview as well. In North Africa the Long-Range Desert Group (LRDG), the Special Air Service (SAS), and Popski's Private Army all carried out operations behind German lines, often against the tenuous logistics lines or against the Luftwaffe airfields. The Germans did return the favour to a smaller extent as they formed their own version of the Long-Range Desert Group from personnel with desert experience.

Other British special operations units were geared towards raids or intelligence gathering along coast lines. Combined Operations Pilotage Parties (COPPs), for example, gathered information necessary for amphibious landings. The Special Boat Section (SBS) was another unit formed to carry out operations using the Klepper canoe. The SBS while operating as part of the SAS in the Mediterranean and Adriatic would prove especially effective. In the Far East, Middle East Commando carried out raids and intelligence gathering operations, while the Chindits operated as a long-range penetration unit.

This array of British special operations forces also helped engender other European units as Free French, Belgians, Dutch, Poles, Norwegians, and others served with the Commandos or SAS. In many cases, these personnel formed the cadre for their country's special forces after liberation from the Germans. One of the most interesting of these foreign contingents serving with the British was X Troop of #10 Inter Allied Commando. X Troop was comprised of native German speakers, including German Jews, and was used for many dangerous missions.

Many of the US special operations forces of World War II also owe their formation to their British counterparts. The Rangers and USMC Raiders

Special operations personnel will often work with local partisans such as this one in Greece during World War II (BA).

both were influenced by the British Commandos. Both, in fact, sent personnel to train with the Commandos and bring back the lessons learned. The US combat swimmer unit, the Underwater Demolition Teams (UDTs), evolved because the US was engaged in so many amphibious operations in the Pacific as well as in Europe, but at least some lessons were learned from the experiences of COPPs. Two US units which evolved separately from the British experience were both trained for mountain and ski warfare. The 10th Mountain Division was a special operations unit only in the sense that it was trained for operations in 'special' terrain. The First Special Service Force, however, was a true special operations unit. Originally formed for raids in Norway using tracked 'Weasels' (supply carriers), the Force would eventually be trained for airborne, amphibious, ski and mountain warfare. OSS Operational Groups were trained to operate behind enemy lines and form guerrilla forces, a mission which has become standard for special operations units.

Other World War II combatants had units which carried out special missions. For the Japanese, the airborne troops and Special Naval Landing Force (SNLG) could be employed for special missions. The Soviet Union employed its airborne troops in an interesting fashion which gave them a substantial special operations capability. Although usually deployed in multi-battalion or divisional drops, Soviet airborne forces normally reverted to the role of partisans after the drop, often augmenting partisan forces operating in the area. NKVD special units carried out other assignments behind German lines including intelligence gathering and assassination.

After World War II, many of the special operations units which had been formed were disbanded, including the SAS, but within a few years the rising tide of Marxist insurgences offered numerous venues for the employment of special operations units. During the Korean War, the US Army Rangers, now airborne-qualified, and the British Commandos were used for raiding missions. Along the North Korean coast US UDTs were used as well. For more unconventional operations, units such as the United Nations Partisans in Korea (UNPIK) operated behind North Korean lines.

In Indochina, the French made great use of airborne troops and naval commandos, but the true special operations unit was the Groupement de Commandos Mixtes Aeroportes (GCMA). This unit carried out the classic special forces mission of raising guerrillas to fight against the Viet Minh. Drawing from tribesmen in the mountainous areas of northern Vietnam, the GCMA proved an effective force multiplier.

British special forces personnel, especially the SAS, which had been re-constituted as a regular regiment in Malaya, proved very effective in counter-insurgency campaigns in Malaya, Aden, Oman, and Borneo. Royal Marine Commandos would be employed in some of these operations as well. Other British special operations units, including the SBS, were assigned to the British Army of the Rhine for operations against the Soviets should they invade Western Europe.

By the Korean War era in the USA, the World War II OSS had provided the basis for the Central Intelligence Agency (CIA) and the US Army Special Forces. The original 10th Special Forces Group would evolve into Special Forces Groups targeted at Europe, Asia, Latin America, Africa, and the Middle East. It was in Southeast Asia that the US Army Special Forces would first see extensive use, primarily in South Vietnam but also in Laos, Thailand, and Cambodia. Other US Special Operations forces which would see significant service during the Vietnam War included the Navy's Sea, Air, Land (SEAL) Teams, the Air Force's Combat Control Teams (CCTs), and the USMC Recons. Special forces from Thailand, South Vietnam, South Korea, the Philippines, Australia, and New Zealand would be deployed against the Communist insurgents as well. Although many of the US special operations personnel would be deployed training indigenous troops such as the Montagnards, others were assigned to

An SAS patrol in Northern Europe demonstrates proper security during movement (21 SAS).

Military Assistance Command Vietnam/Special Operations Group (MACV/SOG) or other reconnaissance units. Another group primarily comprised of Navy SEALs was involved in riverine operations, particularly in the Mekong Delta. The Phoenix Program which targeted the Viet Cong infrastructure also employed a substantial number of special operations personnel.

Surrounded by enemies intent on its destruction, Israel has found it necessary to rely on its special operations forces to carry out a wide array of operations, particularly during periods of 'low intensity warfare'. The General Staff Deep Recon Unit 262 was formed in 1958 and was used for operations into Lebanon. Israeli special operations units have put great stress on counter-terrorist training and have been involved in many such operations, the most famous of which was the raid on Entebbe Airport to free Israeli hostages.

Other counter-terrorist units were formed as a result of acts of terror directed against the Israelis. After the 1972 massacre of Israeli athletes at the Munich Olympics, many countries created units specifically tasked

France's 2nd REP is trained as a special ops unit which can be quickly deployed anywhere in the world (ECP).

with countering aircraft hijackings and other hostage incidents. Among the best known of these units are France's GIGN, Germany's GSG-9, and the USA's Delta Force. Other established special operations units such as the SAS added counter-terrorism to their brief.

In the Soviet Union, the *Spetsnaz* units of the GRU had been used for special operations since World War II, but it was the war in Afghanistan that illustrated the need for a special operations capability to hunt and ambush guerrillas. The Soviets also established naval *Spetsnaz* units as well as KGB special operations units sometimes known as *osnaz*, which were used for politically sensitive missions.

The French took a very interesting and very French approach to at least part of their special operations capability. Once the North African and Indochinese colonies had achieved independence, the French Foreign Legion no longer had their traditional areas of operation. After the 1st Legion Parachute Regiment had revolted in Algeria and been disbanded, only the 2nd REP (Foreign Legion Parachute Regiment) remained as a Legion airborne unit. Since France has never been hesitant about using the Legion as opposed to French troops for dangerous operations, it seemed only logical to train the 2nd REP for an array of special operations including High-Altitude Low Opening (HALO), mountain, small boat, etc. The resulting unit, based on Corsica, could be used for deployment anywhere in the world in all environments.

Special operators assigned to counter-terrorism find that parachuting skills are still useful for insertion and building confidence. In this case members of France's GIGN counter-terrorist unit show their equipment for parachuting, scuba, etc. (ECP).

By the 1980s, major powers were using their special operations forces primarily for counter-terrorism, military advisory missions, drug suppression, extraction of their nationals from trouble spots, and other missions where a major military commitment was neither feasible or desirable. Virtually every country in the world by that point had some unit with a special operations mission, often primarily orientated towards internal security. The training of these units usually offered a method for major countries to continue to wield influence through sending their 'more sophisticated' special operations personnel to train friendly 'allies'. Major powers often did exchange training as well to share expertise. Among most Western powers, for example, constant personnel exchanges not only increased expertise but made it much easier for multinational special operations personnel to work together should the mission require it.

In the Falklands War, the SAS and SBS, as well as the Royal Marines Mountain and Arctic Warfare Cadre, had a chance to display their skills in a combat environment, while British special operations personnel have also seen substantial use in Northern Ireland. What was especially interesting in the Falklands War was that members of the SAS found themselves performing the same mission in the frozen South Atlantic that they had performed in the Western Desert during World War II, that is, destroying enemy aircraft on the ground.

US special operations personnel saw action in an abortive attempt to rescue hostages in Iran, though Delta Force never really got the chance to show whether they could carry out the rescue as the mission was aborted because of problems with helicopters. US Rangers, Special Forces, and SEALs were used in the Grenada and Panama invasions, though some problems in the Grenada operations highlighted the need for a Special Operations Command to coordinate special operations.

The end of the Cold War allowed both Russian and NATO special operations forces to receive new missions more in tune with the state of the world. The Gulf War of 1991 saw special forces from many countries involved in a myriad of operations. Saudi, Kuwaiti, and other Middle Eastern special forces units worked closely with the SAS and US Special Forces on missions into occupied Kuwait and later into Iraq, though deep penetration missions were carried out primarily by the Special Forces and SAS. Scud-hunting missions became a major focus for special operations personnel in an attempt to keep Israel from taking unilateral action. Special Forces and SAS personnel also used laser targeting devices to help guide in some 'smart' weapons.

After the Gulf War, special forces were used on some questionable operations as part of 'peacekeeping' forces. Attempts to capture war criminals in the former Yugoslavia or warlords in Somalia were often launched with poor planning and inadequate support. As a result, valuable special operations assets were endangered and, in the case of US Rangers in Somalia, squandered for little gain. On the other hand, special operations units need employment to stay sharp which is often the argument used in favour of employing them on drug suppression or other law enforcement missions.

The current 'War on Terrorism' has offered innumerable opportunities for the use of special forces. Well suited for surgical strikes against terrorist targets, special operations units have been the weapon of choice for missions to kill or capture terrorist leaders in many parts of the world. In Afghanistan and Iraq, US Special Forces and the British and Australian SAS have worked very well raising indigenous forces among the Northern Alliance and the Kurds, while other special operations personnel have carried out the hunt for terrorist leaders, often calling in air strikes once a

US special operations personnel find that skills in handling mules or other livestock often has proven valuable in Afghanistan. These members of Merrill's Marauders during World War II found the mule invaluable as well (USNA).

high-value target has been located. Many other countries have contributed special operations personnel to the conflicts in Afghanistan and Iraq. For example, Poland's GROM, a highly trained special operations and counter-terrorist unit, performed extremely well during the war in Iraq. Afghanistan, particularly, has lent itself to the use of special operations units who can work with indigenous tribesmen and operate in harsh terrain for extended periods. The ability of special operations personnel to call in precision air strikes gives them a combat effectiveness far out of proportion to their numbers, thus making them an invaluable tool in the hunt for al-Qaida and the Taliban.

Combat in Afghanistan has, in fact, offered a good indicator of how special operations forces are likely to be used in the immediate future. Terrorists and/or insurgents are difficult to engage with conventional forces, but small, mobile special operations units can track terrorist groups and either ambush them or pinpoint their location for airmobile forces or air strikes. Often when carrying out such counter-terrorist operations, a large force of Western troops would create unrest in the host country, but a small group of special operators trained to blend with local troops and able to speak the language is an invaluable adjunct to local forces. In such scenarios, the special operations forces will have the capability of operating sophisticated equipment which can assist local forces in their mission or will be able to provide satellite or communications intercepts which can speed response if a high-value terrorist target is located.

Perhaps the easiest way to summarise the special operations mission is to list the missions which currently fall under the purview of the US Army Special Forces:

- countering the proliferation of Weapons of Mass Destruction (WMDs)
- counter-terrorism
- assistance to foreign countries in internal security and defence
- covert reconnaissance and intelligence gathering
- direct action to seize or destroy enemy personnel or hardware
- psy ops (psychological operations)
- civil Affairs to help win hearts and minds
- unconventional or guerrilla warfare
- counterinsurgency
- disruption of enemy communications systems and command and control
- liaison or support in coalition warfare
- combat search and rescue
- drug interdiction
- humanitarian assistance during natural disasters or other disruptions
- assistance in training foreign personnel on US equipment
- provide a special operations capability for 'peace-keeping' operations
- black operations including assassinations and snatches

Special operations forces tend to comprise long-service professionals who are highly motivated and highly trained. Their place in contemporary warfare seems to be assured, but caution must be exercised in expanding special operations forces so that quality of selection and training is not compromised. Care must also be taken that these valuable assets are not squandered in missions which require heavier forces.

Chapter 2

Selection and Training

Although some special operations units allow direct enlistment, normally the maturity and experience gained by having served a few years in more conventional military units is a prerequisite. However, exceptions may be made for personnel with particularly desirable skills. An officer with a degree in nuclear engineering or biochemistry, for example, might be a highly desirable recruit for a unit tasked with tracking and destroying WMDs. Likewise, those whose appearance and language skills would allow them to pass as locals in certain societies might be fast-tracked into certain special operations units. Generally, however, a few years of prior military service is highly desirable for the special operations recruit.

Selection criteria
Exactly what prior service is best for those who join special operations units offers some area of discussion. Traditionally, service in airborne units has been the most common as the tough physical training and the experience at parachuting will prove useful. On the other hand, helicopter pilots, military engineers, signals specialists, linguists, intelligence specialists, medics, and those with various other specialisms can add diversity to the special operations unit.

There are also various theories about what type of civilian background best moulds the potential special operations soldier. Generally, someone who is athletic and likes the outdoors makes a prime candidate. However, the special operations soldier also needs a sound intellect so either academic ability or a deep interest in reading and study are usually appealing traits as well. Because special operators often find themselves in situations where they will be working with horses, sheep, cattle, or other animals employed by indigenous personnel with whom they will interact, a background on a farm or ranch can be useful though is certainly not necessary. One of the best SAS soldiers of the author's acquaintance grew up in London yet became an expert on outdoor survival. There is also a theory that a background in carpentry or other construction trades can be useful since special operations soldiers may be employed on 'hearts and minds' campaigns. These or other civilian backgrounds may have some value, but far more important is the ability to learn diverse skills quickly, thus allowing the city-bred special operator to become adept in the wilds and the country-bred special operator to learn the ability to shadow a suspected terrorist in the world's largest cities.

Most units use some type of pre-selection programme to eliminate those who lack basic skills. Such programmes usually incorporate intelligence tests and psychological profiles, physical fitness tests, often including a swimming test, and a firearms qualification course. In the US Army Special Forces, for example, the Special Forces Assessment and Selection (SFAS) covers twenty-four days during which up to two-thirds of the candidates are eliminated. Generally, instructors will be observing those in pre-selection to determine which candidates they feel will have a chance actually to make it through the rigorous selection procedure. Those deemed likely candidates will be invited to attend the next selection course and will probably be encouraged to work on their physical condition.

The actual selection courses normally combine tests of basic military skills with tasks which require individual or team initiative. Long runs and hikes with equipment are designed to test the candidate's commitment to completing the selection course as well as his stamina. What are often called 'sickeners' are added to give the candidate a chance to quit. In fact, he is often encouraged to quit. For example, after completing a particularly long march, candidates may be told that the transport which was expected to take them back to the base failed to arrive so they will have to march back. This offers an easy chance for some to collapse with fatigue and declare they cannot go in. Usually those who continue and begin the march back find the transport a short distance down the road.

Delta Force and the SAS use many of the same selection techniques. Great stress is put on the ability to follow instructions and skill in land navigation. Exercises often include being required to make a rendezvous on time, usually with only minimal instructions about what is required. The lack of set instructions and a predetermined schedule often eliminates excellent military personnel who have trouble adjusting to the lack of the rigid structure to which they are accustomed. The final selection will be based upon the ability to navigate a tough course between various checkpoints in a set amount of time.

The SAS incorporates other aspects intended to put the responsibility

When members of the SAS learn land navigation they also learn techniques such as using a stalk of grass to point at a map so no indications are left for enemy intelligence to spot.

for success upon the individual. For example, on many orienteering marches, only sketch maps prepared by the candidate will be allowed. For those used to printed military topographical maps, this can prove daunting. The SAS and most other special operations units keep increasing the length of runs or marches as the selection course progresses, with times expected to be lower and lower. One of the best-known aspects of the SAS selection course traditionally has been the twenty-four-kilometre run with a full rucksack up Pen-y-Fan. Some SAS marches are as long as sixty-four kilometres, always against the clock. The final slog which must be completed to successfully finish selection covers sixty kilometres over rugged terrain often in harsh weather. Carrying a twenty-five-kilogramme pack, the prospective SAS soldier must complete the march in twenty hours or less.

Other selection courses may incorporate tasks that require creative teamwork to complete them. The need to transport heavy loads over long distances or across chasms has traditionally been one of these initiative tests. Interviews in front of a selection board may also be a way of testing self-confidence and reasoning ability. Often each country will incorporate selection elements which reflect the culture. France's GIGN, for example, has tested the ability to overcome instinctive fears by having personnel lie on the bottom of the Seine for hours while barges pass just a few feet overhead.

Rhodesia's Selous Scouts operated virtually as guerrillas, often living off of the land; hence, their selection course incorporated food deprivation while a dead monkey hung in the middle of the camp rotting away. Once it reached a particularly ripe state, it was cooked and fed to the ravenous candidates. Not only did this act as a 'sickener' factor to weed out the more queasy, but it also taught some important bush survival lessons,

Selous Scouts undergoing selection pause for a much needed break (David Scott-Donelin).

Members of the Special Air Service on operations in the jungle; washing mess gear is important to maintain hygiene, but note that one man remains on constant guard against ambush.

including the fact that maggots actually add protein and decomposing meat can be eaten if properly cooked, but it cannot be reheated. Many aspects of special operations selection, including the Selous Scouts's rotting monkey, were intended to teach valuable lessons.

At least a part of the selection process seems to be the psychological effects of seeing others fail each day and disappear from the course. This

Special ops personnel must be trained to deal with local wildlife and to kill and eat it when necessary. This US Army Ranger demonstrates how the name 'Snake Eaters' arose (US Army).

Combat swimmers are trained to come over a beach for raids or for hydrographic recon (USNA).

helps increase the stress as each candidate wonders if he will be the next to leave. Perhaps this aspect of the selection process is intended to simulate the stress of combat where one never knows when he might be hit, stress that is increased by seeing others fall. Even if this stress is not intended to be comparable with real losses in combat, it does test the candidate's ability to keep going. In coping with the stress of selection, the ability to remain focused on the goal – completion of the task and the course – is a key element, one which helps future special operators complete missions under trying conditions. Not only does completing a rigid selection course train the special operations soldier to cope with difficulties, it also builds his confidence so that he can overcome obstacles to completing his mission.

Although it might be argued that the entire selection process is psychological as well as physical, most units incorporate separate formal psychological testing. In the case of the written psychological tests, candidates are evaluated not just on their answers but upon their ability to maintain concentration despite being fatigued. Falling asleep while taking the tests can result in elimination.

Delta Force has incorporated peer-evaluation as well, in which members who have completed selection rate other members on their leadership, reliability, etc. These ratings help determine how well a candidate will be accepted by those with whom he may be assigned to work.

Another aspect that mimics a situation which arises in combat is the need to keep going despite pain and injury. The difficulties encountered in a selection course will tax even those in the best of condition. Bruises, blisters, strains, sprains, abrasions, and various other injuries are likely to occur, yet the candidate must force himself to keep going in order to pass.

Combat swimmer units such as the US Navy SEALs or Royal Marines SBS incorporate some of the same selection factors as other special operations courses but also have their own distinct flavour. To give some idea of the physical condition deemed necessary even to attempt SEAL training, here is the Basic Underwater Demolition/SEAL (BUD/S) screening test:

- 500-yard swim using the breast- or side-stroke, to be completed in twelve and a half minutes or less
- forty-two press-ups minimum in two minutes
- fifty sit-ups minimum in two minutes
- six dead-hang pull-ups minimum
- one-and-a-half mile run wearing boots and long pants to be completed in eleven and a half minutes or less

BUD/S is broken into three phases: the First Phase emphasises physical conditioning, the Second Phase diver training and the Third Phase land warfare. For the SEALs, BUD/S First Phase combines extreme physical exertion, extensive exposure to water and cold and tasks requiring teamwork, all combined to exert extreme mental and physical pressure. The final 'Hell Week,' which incorporates extremely hard physical tasks with only a few hours' sleep throughout the entire process is designed to eliminate all but the most committed and generally reduces the already diminished class to half or less. Though hard physical conditioning remains a constant in SEAL training, the Second Phase is devoted to learning swimming techniques which will provide the basis for later combat-swimmer training. For example, SEAL trainees learn long-distance swimming techniques using a modified sidestroke that will work well with fins. Since many SEAL operations are carried out under water,

BUD/S trainees learn to swim underwater without breathing apparatus using techniques such as going deep early, since the increased pressure on the oxygen in the lungs will actually let them last longer without having to surface. 'Drown-proofing' with wrists and ankles bound is another aspect of the swimming portion of BUD/S. The Third Phase of BUD/S teaches weapon skills, small-unit tactics and immediate action drills as well as the basics of demolition. Unlike special operations candidates in other services, few SEALs have backgrounds as infantrymen; therefore, the Third Phase of BUD/S is important in preparing them for the more sophisticated land warfare training which will follow.

Once the new SEAL has completed BUD/S he will then go on to eighteen weeks of SQT (SEAL Qualification Training) followed by three weeks of cold-weather training on Kodiak Island. Even after completing all of this training, the SEAL will still receive other specialised training as well as team training once assigned to a unit.

Currently, in an attempt to save money, SAS and SBS selection is combined, but in the past SBS selection was separate. Among the special aspects of SBS selection was an exercise in which candidates were dropped off in their underwear and given a roll of hessian. From his they had to construct clothing, then they had to transport a bomb-trolley carrying a cardboard box 350 miles to the Portland Naval Base by the next day. Initiative exercises such as these test not only dedication but also creative thinking. SBS candidates do three or four dives per day as well as other tough physical training. During their small-boat phase in Scotland, they carry Klepper canoes up and down hills, then conclude with a thirty-mile individual paddle on Loch Long.

Skills training

Once candidates for most special operations units have passed their basic selection they move on to what the SAS calls 'continuation training'. In general terms, this training is designed to provide each special operations soldier with general skills necessary to carry out the missions he will be assigned and to start learning the team skills necessary to become part of a unit.

Although different units provide parachute training at different points during the process, airborne training is standard for virtually every special operator. Because many applicants for special forces come from airborne units, a substantial number of candidates will already have undergone basic static-line parachute training. However, since some applicants come from 'leg' infantry units, engineers, or other military specialities which do not require parachute training, any selectees who are not parachute-

The ability to survive off the land is an important special ops skill.

qualified go through a basic course. Static-line parachute training is usually completed in a few weeks and requires a certain number of qualifying jumps. In the British Army it has traditionally been eight jumps, while the US Army has usually only required five.

Members of the Australian SAS practise proper patrolling techniques. Note that they are well spaced so a single machine-gun burst or mortar round will not take out the entire patrol (Australian War Memorial).

Another aspect of continuation training is survival. Since special operations soldiers will operate in all types of terrain and weather, they must know how to survive and fight in jungle, desert, or mountain conditions. As many of their missions will require them to operate behind enemy lines, they must also learn to avoid capture and resist interrogation.

The experiences of Chris Ryan and Andy McNab of the SAS Bravo Two Zero Patrol in the Gulf War of 1991 graphically illustrate the value of this training as Chris Ryan managed to evade capture and reach the Syrian border while Andy McNab and other members of the patrol evaded initial capture and survived very harsh interrogation. Other SAS personnel captured by the Argentines in the Falklands War found their training in surviving interrogation extremely useful.

Another aspect of this training is escape and evasion, often called 'E & E' in special operations jargon. The US Army Special Forces escape and evasion programme was originally established by Nick Rowe, a Special Forces officer who had escaped from captivity in Vietnam. Escape and evasion programmes teach methods of escape as well as techniques for moving away from the enemy without being tracked. Along with escape and evasion, combat survival will often be taught as well. A combat survival course will teach the special operations soldier to find food, water, shelter, and other necessities.

For the US Army Special Forces, those who have made it through the SFAS will enter one of four Special Forces Qualification Courses (SFQCs) run each year. Phase I lasts thirty-nine days and stresses the basic skills of the light infantryman. Since some candidates may be from non-infantry units they will have to work especially hard to master skills that other candidates will be refreshing. Patrolling, land navigation, and field craft are especially emphasised in this portion of the 'Q Course'. Phase II deals with specialist team skills and will vary in length depending upon the speciality. Officers, for example, spend six months in this phase, while medical specialists can take up to a year which includes rotations in big city emergency rooms. As a result, normally, candidates will not enter Phase III with those from their Phase I group. Phase III emphasises unconventional warfare and ends with a large-scale field exercise simulating the formation of a guerrilla force and other missions. Air operations will normally be covered in this phase as well. By the time a Special Forces soldier has completed the SFQC he will have cost the government not just a year in time but over $100,000 in training costs.

Building skills additionally in weapons and unarmed combat will play an important part in continuation training. Those who have been selected for special operations training will have basic military weapons skills, but the special operator may well be issued with special weapons for clandestine missions (e.g., suppressed firearms). Stress will also be put on developing Close Quarters Battle (CQB) skills, including rapid engagement of multiple targets, malfunction clearance drills, and firing short

Long-range marksmanship skills are invaluable for the special operator (Dan Meany).

Martial arts techniques prepare the special operator for silent elimination of an enemy or to keep fighting if disarmed. All Korean special forces are highly skilled in the martial arts (USNA).

bursts from the sub-machine gun or double taps from the handgun. 'Immediate Action Drills', which will allow a small unit to disengage from an ambush while delivering fire, are generally included as well.

Unarmed combat and use of the fighting knife will stress the silent elimination of enemy personnel or last ditch techniques if one's weapon has been lost or malfunctions. Although most special operations units do not spend too much time on close combat with blades, impact weapons, or hands and feet, normally the basics of such combat are taught. Many special operators will continue such training on their own and reach black-belt status. In specialised counter-terrorist units where such skills may be particularly applicable, martial arts training will be a key element of both initial and continuation training. Generally, special operations units want martial arts training which is especially applicable to their missions. They want techniques which allow them to move rapidly from

Special ops medics can not only give needed care to their teammates but can also help win hearts and minds by treating locals (USNA).

just controlling a prisoner to killing him quickly if necessary. Knife-fighting techniques will concentrate on sentry elimination as well as 'fight to the death' dirty tricks against an armed or unarmed opponent. Although different units may train primarily in one martial art, generally it is best to learn a combination of strikes, blocks, chokes, throws, arm bars, blade techniques, and impact weapon manipulation.

Since special operations units will be deployed worldwide on diverse missions, skills in communication are of great importance. As a result, as part of his continuation training, each special operator will be trained to a high level as a signaller. In addition to traditional basics such as Morse code, special operations 'commo/signals' training will include use of a diverse group of radios, including sophisticated satellite communications systems. An important element of commo training is learning how to calculate the size of antenna necessary to send the signal and how to construct antennae. Special operations messages will generally be encoded and/or sent with burst transmissions. As a result, each operator learns the basics of encoding and decoding messages.

An irony of special operations engineering training is that personnel are trained to construct and de-construct with equal facility. Since units such as the US Army Special Forces are frequently involved in 'hearts and minds' campaigns in which they attempt to win indigenous people over by helping build bridges, roads, wells, schools, or hospitals, they must possess a wide array of building skills, though for major projects they will enlist the help of dedicated engineer units. On the other hand, special operators may be deployed behind enemy lines to carry out acts of sabotage which require knowledge of demolition, including the construction of improvised explosive devices and booby traps.

Also, as special operations personnel often operate far from medical facilities, they receive substantial emergency medical training. The more intensive training given to special forces medical specialists will be covered later under specialist training, but each special operator understands the basics of stabilising an injured comrade. Another aspect taught to US special operations personnel is Tactical Combat Casualty Care (TCCC). Based on an analysis of lives lost and lives saved in combat, TCCC stresses the tactical aspects of emergency medical stabilisation as well as the medical ones. Operators are taught that they may first have to gain fire superiority before they can tend to the casualty, since they and the casualty may continue to be in danger. Then, they must get the casualty to cover before actually beginning to work on him. The highest priority is to stop bleeding since so many casualties die from loss of blood. It may also be necessary to decide who can and who cannot be saved so that efforts will be concentrated on those who can be stabilised and evacuated to a field medical care unit.

One of the most critical skills for special forces personnel is multilingualism. Frequently deployed to work with indigenous personnel, the special operations soldier must be able to communicate and understand the culture of those with whom he works. The US Army Special Forces organises its Special Forces Groups (SFGs) according to the area of the world in which they will operate and gives language training accordingly. For example, the 10th SFG (Airborne, Abn) has traditionally trained for operations in Europe and, thus, has 'A Teams' with expertise in Russian, German, French, and other European languages. The 5th SFG (Abn) has assumed great importance over the last decade since it specialises in the Middle East and has 'A Teams' that speak Arabic, Farsi, various Afghan dialects, etc. Other SFGs specialise in Asia, Latin America, and Africa and speak the appropriate languages. The amount of time needed to achieve basic proficiency in a language will normally vary according to the language. Since members of the 1st SFG (Abn) must learn Asian languages, it will take them longer to achieve basic proficiency than members of, say, the 7th SFG (Abn) who will learn Spanish or Portuguese. So much do members of the these Special Forces A Teams immerse themselves in the cultures in which they will operate that it is very common for them to take wives of the ethnic background of the area in which they specialise.

The Special Air Service also puts great stress on linguistic ability. Traditionally, Arabic, Malay, Swahili, and other languages applicable to likely areas of operations were emphasised, but the Falklands War found the SAS short of Spanish speakers, so language training was broadened considerably. The deployment of SAS personnel to counter drug operations in South America helped develop facility in Spanish as well. The US 5th SFG encountered a similar problem when they were deployed to Afghanistan. They had been trained for operations in the Middle East, so most of them spoke Arabic, the language considered most likely to be of use. But most members of the Northern Alliance spoke Dari, a language not standard for the Special Forces. Some members of the 5th Group spoke Russian, so they could sometimes find a Russian speaker among Northern Alliance personnel to translate. Still, the lesson to be learned is that no matter how carefully languages are specified for special operations units, they may end up fighting elsewhere.

Although it is a skill often associated with the SAS, clandestine surveillance training is important with all special operations units. Special operations personnel must be able to infiltrate positions where they can observe enemy troop movements, command centres, critical installations, or other 'high value' targets. They may report on enemy activity or call in air strikes or artillery on enemy positions. In order to carry out such missions, special operators must learn to construct a hide to blend into the local terrain and must also learn to wait patiently in this hide for days or even weeks.

Normally, members of the special operations units will receive more intensive training in one or two areas. For example, on a US Army Special Forces twelve-man Operational Detachment A (ODA), there will be a commanding officer, an executive officer (normally a warrant officer), and ten sergeants trained as specialists. Each of the ten NCOs receives cross-training in a second specialism so the team can be split yet maintain its ability to perform diverse missions. The five basic areas of training include medicine, engineering, communications, weapons, and administration and intelligence.

Special Forces medical specialists receive a high degree of training and normally spend time in big city trauma centres dealing with gun and knife wounds as part of their training. They also learn the basics of dentistry, pediatrics and child delivery, veterinary medicine, pharmacology, preventative medicine, and health education. These skills allow them to establish clinics for indigenous people with whom they are working or to

Selous Scouts learning to fire enemy weapons (David Scott-Donelin).

assist doctors assigned to work with them. In some cases, doctors specifically assigned to Special Forces will run clinics with the assistance of Special Forces medics. Much of the training for Special Forces medics as well as for those from the Rangers, SEALs, and Air Force Pararescue takes place at the US Army Joint Special Operations Medical Training Center (JSOMTC) at Fort Bragg. This sophisticated facility includes operating theatres, laboratories, an X-ray suite, and an anatomy and physiology lab where the trainees work on corpses. Trainees work with a state-of-the-art computerised patient which can be programmed to display symptoms of various illnesses or injuries. The 'patient's' vital signs will respond to proper treatment. The JSOMTC also has an excellent medical library and computer facilities for access to medical data bases. Many of the doctors assigned have a background in special operations which allows them to tailor instructions to situations that medics are likely to encounter in the field. Once assigned to their units special operations medics can return for additional training in areas such as cardiac life-support or trauma life-support.

The engineering specialists learn to build using basic tools and indigenous personnel. The weapons specialists usually specialise in heavy or light weapons, though they will often be cross-trained in both. Specialists in heavier weapons can train indigenous personnel to use mortars or even light artillery, while the light weapons specialists are skilled in constructing ranges and training in small arms. A Special Forces Company will normally include six ODAs, one of which specialises in HALO (High-Altitude Low Opening), HAHO (High-Altitude High Opening), and other specialised techniques. Another ODA will specialise in scuba diving and small boat operations.

In the SAS, there are four basic patrol skills: medicine, communications/ signals, demolition, and languages. Generally, most SAS personnel have two or more of these skills and some who have been with the regiment for some time may have all four. In addition to their patrol skills, members of the SAS also learn their specialised 'troop' skill. Four four-man patrols form an SAS troop, while four troops form an SAS squadron. Troops are trained as 'Boat Troop', 'Mountain Troop', 'Mobility Troop', or 'Air Troop'. The designations are to some extent self-explanatory. Members of the Boat Troop learn amphibious and scuba-diving skills; Mountain Troop learn climbing, skiing, and arctic warfare; Mobility Troop learn desert operations and the use of Land Rovers; and Air Troop learn HALO, HAHO, and other parachuting skills. Should the entire squadron be deployed to an environment in which one troop has particular skills, they will train other squadron members.

A skill important among all special operations units is the under-standing of guerrilla warfare. In many cases, special operations units have been deployed to carry out counter-insurgency operations. In other cases, they raise and train indigenous guerrilla forces. This is the speciality of the US Army Special Forces. In fact, during the defeat of the Taliban and al-Qaida in Afghanistan, as few as one hundred US Army Special Forces soldiers assisted the Northern Alliance in its drive on Kabul. Few scholars are as well-read in the field of guerrilla warfare as members of the Special Air Service or the US Army Special Forces. However, the members of the special operations units study the theory and history of guerrilla warfare in preparation for experiencing it first hand.

In the case of the US Army Special Forces, the war in Afghanistan has illustrated the diverse nature of skills necessary to assist irregulars in combat. Members of the 5th SFG deployed to assist the Northern Alliance against the Taliban and al-Qaida had to use their knowledge of caring for and loading pack mules as well as horsemanship, while retaining the ability to use the most sophisticated laser targeting devices, GPS systems, and communication equipment to call in smart weapons. In some cases smart bombs were called in on Taliban or al-Qaida positions just ahead of a cavalry charge. Afghanistan graphically illustrated that special operations personnel have to be masters of nineteenth-century as well as twenty-first-century warfare.

Warrior skills alone, however, are not sufficient as the Special Forces had to be diplomats in attempting to get various warlords to cooperate against al-Qaida and the Taliban. Once areas were liberated, Special Forces operators also had to fill the civil affairs role by helping establish a police force to keep order and by making arrangements for humanitarian aid to flow.

Another skill members of special operations units which raise and train irregulars must master is the art of teaching. Special operators will have to possess the knowledge and skills which they intend to impart but must also be able to teach indigenous personnel, who may well be illiterate. As a result, a portion of training will be devoted to preparing lesson plans and practising presentations.

Members of special operations units during their careers will undergo a wide array of other training. Because they must be kept constantly sharp and ready for deployment, operators will often be sent on an array of courses to gain useful knowledge but also to give them new challenges to help keep their edge. As a result, team or squadron members may be sent to high-speed driving classes, lock-picking and safe-cracking courses, computer security training, additional language classes, etc. Some personnel may learn to fly fixed wing aircraft or helicopters, while those assigned to counter-terrorist duties will often practise on the simulators for various types of commercial aircraft in case they ever have to pass themselves off as flight crew during a hijack attempt.

Although special operations officers train with their men, they also normally undergo some specialised training which prepares them to lead special operators from the front. SEAL officers, for example, go through specialised training which teaches them to work with special operations units from other services. They are also addressed by members of the special operations community, especially SEALs, who have taken part in successful and unsuccessful operations so that they may learn from that experience. Mission-planning is an important part of special operations officer training, and today includes the use of specialised computer programs which aid in mission-planning and intelligence gathering. Most importantly, special operations officers learn to work as part of a team with highly motivated and highly trained troops yet to maintain the ability to command such men.

Members of special operations units may undergo all kinds of other training, but the key point is that members of such units will undergo constant training designed to keep their abilities at a peak which will let them go directly into combat if necessary. The intensive selection and training process for special operations personnel is such that only a small percentage survive the process and those that do are not fully trained for two years or more. As a result, it is very hard to increase the number of special operations personnel rapidly when needed. In the USA and Great Britain, the pool of manpower in Territorial Army (TA) SAS regiments or National Guard or Reserve Special Forces units allows some flexibility, but as the 'War against Terrorism' and the war in Iraq (2003) have shown, special operations capability can become stretched very quickly. In Afghanistan, for example, two SAS squadrons were committed to one battle, the first time this many members of the SAS had fought together since World War II.

Chapter 3

Weapons and Equipment

The special operations soldier finds himself in a dilemma regarding his weapons and equipment. Because he operates in small numbers often far behind enemy lines or in guerrilla/terrorist controlled territory, he must travel as light as possible. Traditionally he must rely on stealth or, as the SBS motto states, 'not by strength but guile'. Nevertheless, he must be able to deliver sufficient firepower to disengage from contact, escape quickly, and evade. He must also have the means of keeping an enemy at some distance to secure a landing zone for an emergency helicopter extraction. As a result, the special operator's weapons must be chosen to offer a compromise between weight, range, and firepower. Though his individual weapons may be relatively light, however, today's special operations soldier has the ability to call in precision munitions with great accuracy either to prevent being overrun or in support of other missions.

Rifles and accessories

For most special operators, the most basic weapon is the rifle or carbine. For US special operations personnel and some other units the M4 carbine version of the M-16 rifle has proven extremely effective despite its compact size. Its 14.5-inch barrel allows the M4 to be handled very quickly in close quarters or in immediate action drills, yet it still can reach out to 500 metres or more. Many special operators use the M4A1 which has a removable carrying handle to allow the easy attachment of optical sights such as the ACOG, Aimpoint, or ELCAN, the last used on Canadian and Dutch versions of the M4A1. There is also a Special Operations Peculiar Modified Version (SOPMOD) which incorporates handguards with additional rails for mounting lights, lasers, or infrared (IR) illuminators. The Mini Night Vision Sight (MNVS) is a popular addition the SOPMOD M4A1. A special 77-grain .223 load developed by

Some special ops troops from Canada, Denmark, the UK, and other countries use the M-16 with the ELCAN sight and the Beta-C 100-round magazine.

Black Hills Ammunition allows the M4 to perform more effectively at long range, as in the mountains of Afghanistan.

Other versions of the M-16 are also used by US and allied special operations personnel. The M-16A2 is designed as a more accurate and longer-range version of the M-16 and is designed to optimise the 62-grain SS109 round. As the M-16A3, this version has the removable carrying handle and allows easy mounting of optical sights. The M-16A2 has been used by USMC special units among others. The Canadian and Dutch armed forces use the M4A2 and the M-16A3, normally with the ELCAN optical sight. The short-barrelled 'Commando' version of the M-16 is used by Delta Force when assigned to VIP protection details or by other

Special ops units may use the SOPMOD accessories for the M4 carbine, including handguards designed to take lights, lasers, etc. Note also the light and pistol grip as well as the ACOG optical sight.

members of the US special operations units when a very compact weapon of sub-machine gun (SMG) size is desirable. The SAS and SBS both use variations of the M4 or M-16 to suit their mission. Members of the SAS as well as many US special operations units prefer the M4 or M-16 with the M203 grenade-launcher attached.

Among some special operations units, the bullpup assault rifle has proven popular since it combines short overall length with a relatively long barrel. The Steyr AUG has been used by Austrian special operations forces but also by others, including those of Oman and Ireland, who find its compactness and built-in optical sight appealing. The French FAMAS rifle has also been used by French special operations forces as well as the 'special forces' of a few African states. For special operations usage a version of the FAMAS which employs a rail for fitting various optical sights is available.

German and Spanish special operations forces use various versions of the G36 rifle. The G36K, which is the short-barrelled version, is the most popular with special operations forces. In German service the G36K is often issued with the 100-round Beta-C magazine, though it will also take standard M-16 magazines with an adaptor. One of the notable features of the G36 and G36K is a 3x optical sight built into the carrying handle.

The Beretta M12 which is used by some special ops units.

Some Kommando Spezialkrafte (KSK) deployed to Afghanistan have also been seen using the G36C version which has an accessory rail built in to the carry handle and allows the mounting of various optical sights, lights, lasers, etc., instead of the 3x optical sight.

Russian special operations forces as well as many former Soviet Republics use the AK-74 or AK-47. However, the best of the Russian special operations weapons is probably the AKSU, the short version of the AK-74. During the theatre assault in Moscow (October 2002), KGB Alpha Team members used their AKSUs with red dot optical sights, and other specialised sights are available for the AK-74 system of rifles. Russian Spetsnaz also have access to specialised assault rifles or carbines such as the AS silent assault rifle which fires a special subsonic 9 mm round. Some former Warsaw Pact countries which are now in NATO, such as Poland, use rifles or carbines which are derived from the AK-74 but are chambered for the NATO standard 5.56 round.

Although the assault rifle or carbine is by far the most ubiquitous weapon with special operations units because of its versatility, the sniping rifle is also widely used since it allows the special operator to reach out to eliminate an enemy selectively from long range. Two Delta Force snipers, for example, were inserted to hold a horde of Somalis at bay at

A member of the Selous Scouts, a special ops unit trained to blend with the enemy, carries a Russian light machine-gun (David Scott-Donelin).

Mogadishu until they ran out of ammunition. Snipers from the USA, Britain, Canada, Germany, Australia, and other allied countries have selectively eliminated members of al-Qaida and the Taliban in Afghanistan.

Among US special operations personnel, the M21 sniping rifle has proven popular since, being based on the M-14, it allows faster repeat shots and higher magazine capacity than bolt-action rifles. The M40A1 and M24 bolt-action sniping rifles have also seen substantial usage. All three of these rifles are chambered for the 7.62 mm NATO round, but for a longer range anti-personnel and anti-material role, US troops use .50 calibre rifles from Barrett or Harris. In Iraq and Afghanistan these .50 sniping rifles have allowed kills at well over 1,000 metres.

British special forces normally use one of the Accuracy International series of precision rifles for snipers. The PM model with the 'L96A1' military designation was the standard British version and has been used by the Australian and New Zealand SAS as well. The SAS and some other units including Dutch and German special operations forces have also used the AWM in .338 Lapua calibre for longer-range sniping. The AW which is a 'product improved' PM has been adopted by Australia, Italy, Latvia, Sweden, and the Netherlands. For even longer range or anti-material usage, Accuracy International offers the Accuracy International AW50F which is used by the British and Australian SAS. Since special operations personnel often have to carry their weapons into battle on foot, Accuracy International has also developed the AW50FT, which uses titanium to keep the weight down.

French military snipers normally use the FR-F2, though units such as GIGN or RAID may have the PRM UR rifle. Both are good rifles which have been used to good effect by French snipers. One of the most widely used sniper rifles is Steyr's SSG, though it has been superseded with many units. The Swiss SIG SSG2000 and SSG3000 are excellent precision tactical rifles and are widely used among special police units and some military special operations units. German special operations troops may choose between the SG/1 sniper rifle which is based on the G3 and the PSG1. The MSG90 sniper rifle has also seen some usage with German special operations units or special police units such as GSG-9. Many other countries use one or more of the Heckler & Koch sniping variants as well.

Although Heckler & Koch's sniping rifles as well as the US M21 are semi-automatic in operation, the most widely used semi-automatic sniping rifle and possibly the most widely used sniping rifle in the world is the Russian or Chinese Dragunov. Though not as precise as rifles such as the

Accuracy International or US M40, the Dragunov has served well with Russian Spetsnaz units and offers good accuracy with its ten-round magazine and fast reload capability. At least some US special operations units, including the SEALs, have used Dragunovs as well, both for training and as 'deniable' weapons. It is not uncommon, in fact, for special operations units to have available weapons from neutral or enemy countries for use on operations where they do not want their country of origin to be identified.

Sub-machine guns and light machine-guns

Although sub-machine guns do not have the range for many military operations, their high rate of fire and pistol-calibre ammunition often make them a good choice for certain types of raids or for hostage rescue operations. The Heckler & Koch MP5 has been widely used in various configurations including the suppressed version, the MP5SD, and the compact MP5K. A wide array of accessories, including lights, lasers, and infrared illuminators, allows the MP5 to be configured to perform various close combat missions. This closed-bolt sub-machine gun is so accurate that it allows operators to employ it surgically in hostage rescue or prisoner-snatch operations. The MP5 has also proven popular with some special operations support personnel such as helicopter pilots who insert operators or technical personnel assigned to special operations units. Since the standard pistol for most special operations units is a 9 x 19mm, the same calibre as the MP5, this aids logistics.

After the Heckler & Koch MP5, the most popular sub-machine gun with special operations units is almost certainly the Uzi. This Israeli design has been used by dozens of countries and has developed a well-deserved reputation for durability and reliability. Although the original Uzi was a closed-bolt design, both closed- and open-bolt models are now available. The Uzi is most often encountered with folding stock, but many special operations units have found that the version with the fixed wooden stock is easier to shoot accurately.

Although the MP5 and Uzi are predominant among special operations units, other SMGs may be encountered. The Beretta M12 has seen use with Italian and some Latin American special troops. Machine pistols such as the Czech Skorpion have also been used for highly specialised applications. The Fabrique Nationale (FN) P90 has recently attracted interest among special operations units and was used operationally during the hostage rescue operation by Chilean special operations personnel at the Japanese Embassy in Lima. The Russians have developed an assortment of new SMGs, some of which have seen service with the

Spetsnaz or other Russian special troops such as the OMOH or FSB Alpha.

Although special operations units put great stress upon portability, there are times when heavier weapons such as light machine-guns (LMGs) are needed for support or area control. In some instances, there will be special versions of light machine-guns specifically designed to be lighter and easier to handle for special operations troops. The M60E3 LMG, for example, is a far more portable version of the M60 MG. With the fifty- or one hundred-round box magazine, this weapon can be used quite effectively by special operations troops, though it still weighs almost twenty-five pounds. Its front pistol-grip aids in control when being fired from the slung position while advancing. This version was developed primarily for use by the US Navy SEALs, though other units have adopted it. The M249 SAW is lighter and is widely used by special operations troops, but it is chambered for the 5.56 NATO round, while the M60E2 is chambered for the heavier 7.62 NATO round. Among Russian special operations forces, the RPK-74 LMG is probably the most popular, though the 7.62 mm calibre PKM may still be used when a heavier weapon is needed.

Shotguns

Some special operations units find the tactical shotgun a very effective close combat weapon and normally have some in their armouries. The FN 'Tactical' model which is designed so that the stock and sights are similar to the M4 carbine is a good choice since it feels comfortable to those used to the M4. Beretta, Bernardelli, Franchi, and Benelli all make combat shotguns designed for military use, at least some of which take detachable box magazines to aid in rapid reloading. The Russians also make some tactical shotguns which are applicable to special ops. The Saiga with short barrel and detachable magazine is quite effective and the massive KS-23 fires a 4-gauge cartridge which is available in buckshot and anti-vehicular loadings. Reportedly, firing this weapon is so daunting, however, that qualifying with it could be used as a selection course! The standard US combat shotgun is normally the Remington 870 which is used by special operations units around the world. Some US units, however, use the special enhanced 870 from Scattergun Technologies. Among US self-loading shotguns the Remington 11-87P is a good combat choice. Tactically, the shotgun is very effective against vehicles, for sweeping a room or alley, and for destroying high-tech equipment at close range. Special ammunition is available for a wide array of missions.

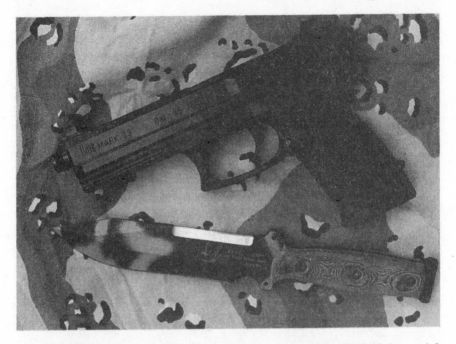

The Mark 23 SOCOM pistol especially developed by Heckler & Koch for special ops troops shown alongside the TOPS BEST knife which is very popular with special ops troops.

Light support weapons

An assortment of light support weapons are in most special operations arsenals, weapons which offer an indirect fire capability or otherwise enhance an operator's lethality. The US M203 40 mm grenade-launcher has already been mentioned and is widely used by units which employ the M-16 or one of its variants. Other countries produce similar grenade-launchers designed for attachment to an assault rifle or carbine, and these may be chosen by special operations forces equipped with weapons from the same source. South Korea's Daewoo K201 grenade-launcher, for example, is often encountered with the Daewoo K2 rifle, while the Russian GP-25 or GP-30 launcher is often encountered on the AK-74. German special operations troops in Afghanistan have been seen using the Heckler & Koch HK69A1 single-shot grenade-launcher, which is well liked because it is so light and handy.

The 40 mm grenades for the M203 grenade-launcher offer the special operator a wide array of options, including high explosive (HE), airburst, buckshot, and illumination. Special operations troops will most likely carry other types of grenades as well. Offensive fragmentation grenades such as the US M61 or British L2A2 are a popular choice, but smoke,

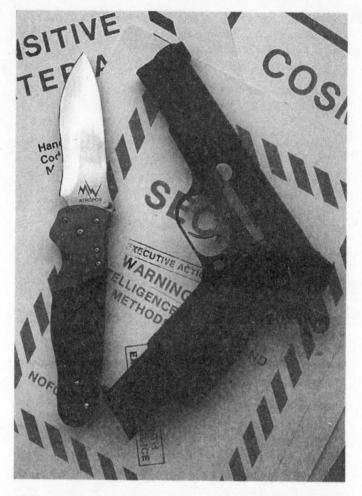

Many special ops units still use the Browning Hi-Power. Versions such as this one custom-built by ROBAR are especially designed for special operations usage. The knife is a folder from MercWorx.

incendiary, concussion, or CS-gas grenades may all have their uses. For hostage rescue operations or snatches of enemy prisoners, stun grenades are in the inventory as well. Although the fact that the M203 may be attached to the M-16 or M4 carbine makes it much more versatile, some special operators still use the M79 single shot grenade.

Some special operations units are willing to pay the price of carrying portable anti-tank weapons, which may be used against armour or against other hardened targets. SAS teams operating behind Iraqi lines during Operation Desert Storm in 1991, for example, often carried some M72 LAWs. The current US light anti-tank weapon, the AT4, does not need to be extended as did the M72 but still has a range of 2,100 metres. Man-portable anti-tank weapons such as the US Stinger may also be applicable to certain special operations missions.

Another weapon which has been popular with many special operations units for decades is the US M18A1 Claymore. This compact command- or trip-wire-detonated anti-personnel device can hurl 700 steel balls into its killing zone and is extremely effective at defending a position or for setting ambushes.

Handguns

Although special operators will normally be equipped with one of the primary weapons discussed above, most will also carry a handgun. Since special operations personnel may be deployed well away from support units, the handgun functions as a reserve weapon in case the primary weapon is damaged or lost. The handgun may also be carried as a secondary weapon with a specialised function (such as being equipped with a suppressor or light). For operators on certain missions, for example, clearing caves in Afghanistan, the handgun may be more handy in closely confined spaces and may be chosen for its quickness of deployment. On counter-terrorist operations, the handgun may be chosen for precise close-range shooting and/or lack of penetration. In some cases, too, special operators will infiltrate areas dressed in native clothing in an attempt to gather intelligence. In such cases, the handgun may be the only weapon they can readily conceal.

Most of the pistols used by special operations units are standard models, perhaps with some minor modifications. The Heckler & Koch Mark 23 SOCOM pistol, however, was developed especially for special operators. This .45 calibre pistol is designed to take a suppressor and has rails for taking specialised illuminators. It also incorporates a recoil reduction system which lowers recoil from the .45 acp cartridge by about thirty per cent. The Mark 23 is a good-sized pistol, especially with the suppressor attached at 16.5 inches.

There are other pistols which have a particular application to special ops. The FN Five-seveN is light in weight due to its polymer frame yet has a twenty-round magazine. Its flat-shooting 5.7 x 28 round is especially effective against body armour. Additionally, the Five-seveN's built-in acces-sory rail allows an assortment of illuminators to be used with the weapon.

For combat swimmer units, certain pistols are designed to operate under water. The Russian SPP-1 is one such pistol which uses four barrels to fire darts under water. The Heckler & Koch P-11 is another underwater pistol which uses multiple barrels – five to be exact. Because the

British special operations forces can trace many of their traditions to the World War II Commandos (IWM).

projectiles normally require a specialised charge, reloads are often carried out by switching a cylinder or other self-contained unit. This aids reload time under water as well, since it limits the number of movements necessary to prepare the weapon for action.

Special ops troops often carry a combination of knives such as this MercWorx Sniper, Extrema Ratio folder, and SOG multi-tool.

Many special operations units use standard military-issue handguns. For decades the most popular was the FN Browning Hi-Power, which offered high reliability and substantial magazine capacity. Some units had their armourers perform work to make the Hi-Power even more accurate, but it is an excellent pistol as issued. Though superseded in many armies, it is still widely used.

The US Colt Government Model .45 auto has also been popular with some special operations units because of its excellent stopping power. Within the US special operations community, marine units such as those assigned to Special Operations Command (SOCOM) or the Marine Expeditionary Unit, Special Operations Capable (MEUSOC) use Government Model pistols which have been tailored to their needs, in some cases incorporating rails for lights, lasers, or other illuminators. The USMC contingent to SOCOM, for example, was issued a special run of Kimber .45 autos. Some special operations units have also chosen the Para-Ordnance or Springfield Armory versions of the Government Model which incorporate a magazine-well for a high capacity fourteen-shot magazine.

Another pistol which has proven very popular with special operations units is the SIG P-226. This pistol incorporates high magazine capacity, double-action first-round capability, and SIG's well-known reliability and accuracy. The latest version of the P-226 incorporates a rail for illuminators making it even more appealing for special operations usage. This pistol is the standard issue weapon for the US Navy SEALs, the Special Air Service and many other units.

The Beretta 92, designated the M9 in US military parlance, is used by some special operators as are variations of the Glock. Although the Makarov PM has been widely used by Russian special forces and those of former Russian republics, newer Russian pistols have begun to replace it. The slim PSM which fires a 5.45 mm round which will penetrate body armour has been issued to some Spetsnaz units, but other pistols such as the PSA which has an eighteen-round magazine capacity and the powerful P-9 Gurza are used by special operators who do not need a concealment pistol.

Since the pistol and sub-machine gun will often be used in Close Quarters Battle (CQB) situations, an important training aid is the Simunitions round and special weapons designed to fire it. Simunitions rounds contain a paint cartridge which will leave a mark on a target that is hit. Although protective masks must be worn when using Simunitions, the use of this training device allows very realistic yet safe man-on-man duelling during training.

Knives

For many special operators the most common anti-personnel weapon they use is the knife. Many special operations units, in fact, issue a distinctive fighting knife as a symbol of the operator's elite status, often awarded upon completion of selection. The Chris Reeve 'Yarborough' or 'Green Beret' is a good example, as is the Extrema Ratio 'Col Moschin'. Both of these are very high-quality knives which will serve an operator for years. Many other special units may be issued traditional knives such as the Fairbairn-Sykes 'Commando Dagger'. The German cutler Eickhorn offers an assortment of fighting knives, many of which have been issued to special operations units. Some specialised knives have been produced for special operators. Titanium knives have been used by some combat swimmer units as have other non-magnetic blades. Specialised sniper knives such as the MercWorx Sniper or the Mad Dog Tactical Utility Sniper's Knife (TUSK) are designed to serve as a fighting knife but will also be effective for building a hide. Mad Dog knives are especially popular in the US special operations community and the Advanced Tactical Assault Knife (ATAK) has seen a great deal of combat usage. For clandestine special operations use, Mad Dog has also supplied the Mirage-X, which is fabricated for missions when a non-metallic knife is needed.

Some special operators prefer to use traditional heavy blades such as the kukri or golok. The SAS, particularly, has always liked the golok, to the extent that the MoD acquires them for issue. Kukris from Himalayan Imports are popular with many US special operations personnel since they are much heavier duty than the kukris usually available as military issue. Latin American special forces have used the traditional hooked banana-harvesting knife as a combat blade, even developing a martial art for its employment.

Other custom knife-makers have developed a long-standing relationship with special operators. Randall in the USA has been supplying combat knives to US special operations troops since World War II. In fact, during the Vietnam War there was a saying that one could always tell a Special Forces soldier because of five possessions: a Rolex watch, a sports car, a star sapphire ring, a Randall knife, and divorce papers!

Most special operators today carry at least one folding knife in addition to a heavy-duty fixed-blade knife. Among those which are popular with special operations personnel are the Extrema Ratio Fulcrum, the Emerson CQC7, and the MoD CQD. The CQD is also available as an automatic knife, a version chosen by some special operations personnel. Other automatic knives which are used by special operations troops include the

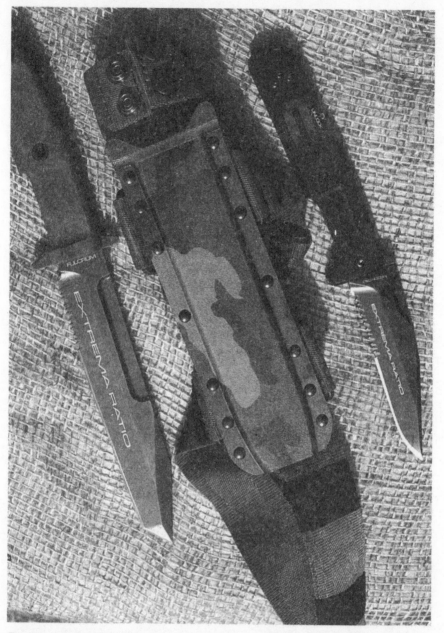

Extrema Ratio fixed-blade and folding knives of the type widely used by special operations troops.

Benchmade AFO and the Microtech QD Scarab. The Czech Mikov and Russian Ladya have also seen use among special operations personnel from the former Warsaw Pact.

Most special operators also carry some type of utility knife or multi-tool. The Swiss Army knife has been a favourite for a long time, with many countries having their own variant. The French, for example, have been issuing the same paratrooper knife since the First Indochina War (1945–54), a knife which incorporates various tools as well as a cutting blade. Polish airborne troops have been issued an automatic knife which has other blades for various tasks. Multi-tools such as those from Leatherman, SOG, and Gerber are popular with US special operations troops. Many, in fact, choose the model with a crimper for use in demolition work.

Explosives

The requirement for demolition work means that most special operations troops have a wide array of explosives and detonators available. Explosives which may be chosen for specific missions might include TNT, Tetrytol, C3, C4, Semtex, Amatol, and PE4. Explosives such as PE4 which are inert unless used with a detonator are the best choice since less care must be taken while transporting them. Special operations personnel also learn to construct improvised explosives from materials such as diesel fuel and chemical fertiliser.

For sabotage missions, various types of detonators are available including timing devices which can run from seconds to years. Such timers may be invaluable for missions where critical materials or personnel are due to be moved into a facility in days or weeks: a device can be placed prior to their arrival, to pre-empt stricter security after they get there. Safety fuse, blasting caps, and detonating cord may also be used to initiate explosive devices. 'Det Cord' is also quite useful when setting ambushes as it may be laid in ditches or elsewhere the enemy might attempt to seek cover. For placing booby traps, initiation devices based upon pressure, motion, closing an electrical circuit, or other means are available.

Normally, special operators all receive basic demolitions training, while specialist personnel receive more intensive training. Operators, for example, learn formulas to determine how much explosive will be needed to destroy various types of targets. Among the types of charges they learn to use are saddle charges, diamond charges, and shaped charges, each designed to optimise the effect in a different situation. For sabotage, special operators learn techniques of dust initiation to use an explosive charge to cause a large explosion in a mill, mine, or other area where dust particles are present. For use on counter-terrorist operations or snatches, operators learn to create frame charges for taking down doors or windows.

A Navy SEAL blends with the jungle; camouflage skills are important in special ops (USNA).

Surveillance and communications equipment

Since intelligence-gathering is such a key element in the special operations mission, surveillance equipment is an extremely important part of the operator's kit. Special operations personnel are also particularly adept at fighting at night so Night-Vision Goggles (NVGs) or similar devices are invaluable for both intelligence gathering and target acquisition. Normally, night-vision equipment will be based on thermal imaging or image intensification. The US AN/PVS-7 Night Vision goggles which have seen use in Afghanistan and Iraq are good examples of equipment light enough for special operations usage. The PVS-7D may be worn on a helmet or used as a binocular. It magnifies ambient light millions of times and also incorporates a small infrared light as well. The Russian 1PN83 night-sight is interesting since it incorporates a laser target-designator as well as night vision technology. The British Pilkington Kite is another night-sight compact enough for special operations usage. For intelligence-gathering, compact video cameras will often be used which can send information back to a command centre in real time. In many cases, these cameras will be combined with a modular system which allows infrared or other specialised components to be fitted to suit the mission. Among more basic night-fighting aids are lights and laser designs to be fitted to rifles, carbines, SMGs, shotguns, or handguns. Insight Technology and SureFire manufacture excellent special operations illuminators.

Many special ops personnel privately purchase boots such as the Desert Acadia from Danner which is specially designed for desert ops.

A USAF Pararescueman prepares for a jump into the sea (USAF).

Since special operators fight at night, they must be able to identify friend or foe when using night-vision equipment. One aid is an infrared transmitter worn by operators so they can be identified by other ground personnel or helicopters. The US Phoenix IR transmitter weighs only two ounces and may be easily worn on the webbed gear yet it can be seen at twenty miles using NVGs. Personnel may also use the survival strobe equipped with an IR cover.

In many cases, the special operator will have equipment which can be used for visual surveillance but when combined with a Global Positioning System (GPS), a laser range-finder, and a laser target-designator can be used to call in precision air strikes, artillery fire, or cruise missile strikes. For combat swimmers a miniature GPS waterproof to twenty metres allows more accurate underwater navigation to a target. The Laser Designator has become a critical piece of special operations equipment since it allows the operator to call in devastating firepower using what the Taliban in Afghanistan called a 'death ray'. The Special Operations Forces Laser Acquisition Marker (SOFLAM) is widely used by US Special Forces while the Pilkington LF25 is used by British special operations personnel. The Pilkington is typical of current man-portable laser designators. Only eight kilogrammes in weight, it allows targets to be 'painted' or 'lased' out to 10,000 metres. The SOFLAM weighs even less at twelve pounds and has a ten-kilometre range. The SOFLAM incorporates a 10x magnification and night-vision optics.

An absolutely essential piece of equipment for special operations troops is a radio. In fact, many special operations units will be equipped with multiple radios which allow them to communicate at different distances and with different degrees of security. The special operations radio must be as compact as possible for troops who must carry all of their equipment as they move on foot yet must be very durable and versatile. One radio used by the SAS, the PRC319, is typical of many pieces of special operations communications equipment. Capable of storing up to twenty channels, it breaks down into four components, is waterproof, and is capable of burst transmissions.

US special operators use a variety of radios to fit the mission. The Raytheon AN/PSC-5 (V) is an example of one which is widely used. Weighing less than twelve pounds without the battery which adds another eight pounds, it is capable of UHF/VHF as well as satellite communications. For communication between members of a unit, the AN/PRC148 weighs less than two pounds yet incorporates a keypad, graphics display, and built-in speaker-microphone. Another US special operations radio is the Thales Miniature Secure Handheld Radio (MSHR) which uses digital design, flash transmission capability, and encryption. It is endorsed by the National Security Agency. For operations in a hostile environment, the Motorola Astro Saber is especially sturdy and also has good encryption capability.

In some situations, special operators do not want to use their radios. When escaping or evading in hostile territory, radio transmissions to search and rescue helicopters might be used to locate the special operator

Small boat skills are very important to special ops personnel.

or the search and rescue personnel. As a result, many operators now are equipped with a Combat Survivor Evader Locator (CSEL). The US PRQ-7 CSEL incorporates a GPS and tracking beacon to allow search and rescue to track the operator with no direct radio contact.

Other equipment

Various other items of kit are important to special operations personnel. Today, backpack hydration systems such as the Blackhawk Hydrastorm allow more water to be carried conveniently than using traditional canteens while offering immediate access to the water via a drinking tube. This allows the operator to drink while continuing to move. Some hydration systems are designed for incorporation into an assault-vest so that basic necessities or survival items can be carried along with the water carrying bladder.

Medical kits are extremely important to special operations personnel. Since special operations units will often operate far from emergency medical treatment in situations which may not allow immediate evacuation in the event of injury, or MedEvac, the special operations medic must be prepared to perform a wide array of medical procedures. Additionally, special operations medics may be called upon to perform medical functions with indigenous civilian populations. As a result, the medical kit must contain such standbys as bandages, splints, chest tubes, tracheotomy kit, intravenous kit, drugs, etc. However, instruments for performing basic surgery and dental procedures are normally included as well.

Special operations troops use some standard uniform items but often incorporate their own specialised items as well. For example, special operations troops will normally forego the standard ballistic helmet, though they may wear helmets for parachute or helicopter insertions and may also use a ballistic helmet for hostage-rescue operations. Frequently, however, they will wear some type of indigenous headgear to help make their silhouette less obviously that of a foreign soldier. Gore-Tex has proven very popular with special operations troops since it offers a high degree of warmth and water resistance while maintaining light weight. Camouflage may be worn but may also be mixed with indigenous clothing. Newer types of camouflage which not only help blend with surroundings but also make it harder to identify the wearer using night-vision equipment are also used by some special operations units. Special operations snipers will incorporate camouflage with a 'ghillie suit' or scraps of local flora.

Perhaps the most important component of the uniform for a special operations soldier is his boots. In some units, in fact, personnel will have a half-dozen pairs of boots, each designed for a special type of mission (e.g., climbing, arctic/winter, desert, etc.). In many cases, because the special operator will be operating on foot for such extended periods, personnel will purchase their own boots or teams will order their own foot gear. In the US special operations community, Danner boots are highly prized and have been used by many foreign special operations units as well. Many are constructed with CROSSTECH from Gore so that they are waterproof and incorporate ProTec non-metallic toes. Their Desert Acadia is specifically designed for operations in the Middle East, while the Striker Side Zip allows another popular boot to be temporarily loosened without having to undo the laces, a very useful feature in units which might have to immediately go into action after a short break.

Gas masks/respirators may not be carried by all special operations personnel, though for hostage-rescue operations where gas or stun grenades may be deployed, masks are invaluable. For cave- or bunker-clearing operations, too, the respirator will be important. Current special operations respirators will normally incorporate lenses which may be used with night vision equipment and will have an internal microphone. Some also incorporate a drinking tube. When respirators are not used, many operators will still use ballistic goggles to protect their eyes. Body armour

The SAS has used vehicles especially set up for desert operations since World War II. Shown here is one of the famous 'Pink Panthers' (22nd SAS).

may be too heavy and bulky for many special operations missions, though some current Kevlar soft body armour may still be worn under indigenous attire fairly easily. Assault body armour will be worn for hostage rescue operations. Even some well-conditioned special operations troops found in the mountains of Afghanistan, however, that climbing was difficult with body armour incorporating a hard plate. Assault vests which allow weapons, ammunition, radios, and other equipment to be carried about the torso are widely used by special operations troops. Some of these vests also incorporate pockets for Kevlar and ceramic-plate body armour.

Combat swimmers have need of a great deal of specialised equipment to enable them to operate under water. Basically, there are three types of breathing apparatus normally used by special operations swimmers. The scuba is an open-circuit, compressed-air system which releases bubbles. As a result, it is not normally used when stealthy approaches under water are desired, normally the case on special operations. More likely to be used is one of the two types of closed circuit systems. The Draeger MK V, which is used by many units uses one hundred per cent oxygen in a rebreather, but it is only safe to about thirty-five feet or less because of the fear of oxygen poisoning. Most combat swimmer operations take place above that, so the MK V is applicable. If, however, a combat swimmer has to operate at a lower depth, units such as the Draeger MK XV are available. A closed-circuit, mixed-gas apparatus, it allows deeper diving.

Along with the breathing apparatus, the swimmers will use either a wet or a dry suit. The wet suit absorbs a layer of water which body heat warms and which acts as insulation. For deeper dives, a dry suit will be used. This type of suit is sealed and allows the wearing of thermal underwear or insulated clothing underneath.

Other pieces of combat swimmer kit include an 'Attack Board' (also known as a 'Compass Board'). Designed to help the swimmer navigate underwater, the attack board is usually of polymer and has attached a watch, compass, and depth gauge. More recent versions may incorporate a GPS system as well. Swimmers also have one or more types of buoyancy-control devices. This might be belts with weights which can be added or removed, or vests which can be inflated or deflated to control the diver's buoyancy at different depths. A dive mask and fins will normally complete the basic equipment for the combat swimmer. For units such as the SBS or SEALs who may swim ashore but then operate on land, waterproof rucksacks to carry equipment securely will normally be used.

Special operators may also reach their area of operations via parachute. Although most receive their initial training with static-line parachutes, mission insertions are far more likely to be via freefall. HALO insertions allow parachutists to drop off an enemy's radar rapidly, then open the 'chute shortly before landing. Normally, a GPS and altimeter will be used for HALO insertions. HAHO insertions are used when the parachutist may have to be dropped some distance from the target (e.g., across a border). For HAHO, a Ram-Air Parachute System is normally used. The SAS GQ360 Ram-Air 'chute, for example, allows an operator to jump from 10,000 metres, then glide for over an hour and cover fifteen miles or more. Altimeters and GPS systems will normally be used on HAHO insertions as well.

For HAHO insertions, members of a patrol or team will normally assemble in the air, then glide to the target together. Because the insertion will begin from a substantial height, an oxygen mask will normally be required by each jumper. To allow assembly in the air, each team member will wear a strobe, possibly with an IR cover, on the helmet. The leader will often have a different coloured strobe to allow assembly on him.

Combat swimmers or other seaborne special operations personnel will often make use of small boats to insert on to an objective. The largest normally considered a special operations boat is the Patrol Boat, Coastal (PBC) used by the US Navy SEALs. Used for interdiction against smugglers, terrorists, or insurgents as well as to insert special operations units, the PBCs normally operate in pairs. 170 feet long and powered by four diesel engines producing 3,350 horsepower, the PBC has a crew of four officers and twenty-four enlisted men. Normally, the commanding officer is drawn from surface warfare officers rather than special ops. The PBC has a maximum speed of thirty knots and is armed with a Mark 38 25 mm rapid-fire gun, a Mark 96 25 mm rapid-fire gun, Stinger AA missiles, and four mounting pintles carrying a combination of M2 .50 MG, M-60 7.62mm MG, and Mark 19 grenade-launcher. This firepower can be very effective in supporting SEALs on raiding missions.

Smaller boats are more the norm for special operations forces since they allow insertion on to the beach, oil rigs, or ships. Among those used by special operations units, the Gemini is especially popular. Both the SAS and the SBS use this inflatable which is available in three sizes, the seventeen-foot version being the largest. A choice of eighteen or forty horsepower engine is available. The most popular inflatable with US special operations forces is the Compact Rubber Raiding Craft (CRRC), better known as the 'Zodiac'. It is fifteen feet overall and employs a fifty-five horsepower engine. There is also the Inflatable Boat, Large (IBL) which is fourteen feet long and will comfortably carry eleven operators. Note that US special operators tend to call all inflatables 'rubber ducks'. More durable in rougher seas is the Rigid-Hull Inflatable Boat (RHIBS), usually known as 'Ribs'. The RHIBS incorporates a fibreglass hull and rigid motor-mount, while the gunwale is inflatable.

The 'Boston Whaler', more officially designated the Patrol Boat, Light (PBL) was first used by the SEALs in Vietnam but continues in service. Fabricated of foam-filled fibreglass, the PBL is twenty-five feet long and employs two 155 horsepower outboard motors. It can be armed with a. 50 or 7.62 mm calibre machine-gun. Another popular boat with special operations forces is the Rigid Raider which incorporates a flat bow which allows it to be driven onto shallow beaches. A lighter Kevlar version of the Rigid Raider is especially popular with special operations forces. Powered by two 140 horsepower motors, the Rigid Raider is very fast which makes it especially useful for fast runs onto a beach for clandestine insertions.

Continuing a World War II tradition, the SBS and SAS still use the Klepper canoe, a two-man collapsible which is seventeen feet long.

The craft already described are designed to insert operators from the surface, but there are also specialised craft designed for combat swimmers who approach their target underwater. The Submersible Recovery Craft used by the SAS and SBS is designed to operate at high speed on the surface and low speed submerged. To accomplish this, it employs a ninety horsepower engine on the surface, and two 24-volt electric motors when submerged. The US Navy SEALs use a MK VIII SEAL Delivery Vehicle (SDV) which is a 'wet' system requiring the SEALs to ride on the exterior of the craft. It is, however, equipped with an on-board breathing system with full face masks, thus allowing the swimmers to save their air tanks for use once they leave the SDV. To aid in reaching the target, the SDV is also equipped with a Doppler computerised navigation system, an obstacle avoidance system, and side-scanning sonar. The SDV travels about twice as fast as an operator can swim and allows his energy to be conserved during an operational approach. The SDV can be used to a depth of 500 feet. The Advanced SEAL Delivery System (ASDS) is a 'dry' conveyance which allows the combat swimmers to ride inside.

For land operations, special operations troops use a variety of light, fast vehicles. One of the most famous is the SAS Land Rover. Traditionally, the SAS has used the long wheelbase version which can carry more on long-range desert operations. The current Land Rover Special Operations Vehicle (SOV) is powered by a turbo-charged diesel and can carry six operators. A wide array of weapons may be mounted or carried on the SOV, including a dual 7.62 mm MG in the 'pulpit' above the driver and navigator. Grenade-launcher, TOW anti-tank missiles, or other armament may be carried as well. The US High-Mobility Multi-Purpose Wheeled Vehicle (HMMWV), usually known as the 'Humvee', is used by US and other special operations troops. In its desert operations version the HMMWV employs enhanced cooling and filtration. The HMMWV can also mount an array of weapons including machine-guns, grenade-launchers, etc.

The First Gulf War in 1991 saw the initial employment of the Light Strike Vehicle (LSV). Basically, a militarised 'dune buggy', the LSV has also been designated the Fast Attack Vehicle (FAV) or Desert Patrol Vehicle (DPV). Normally configured for either two or three passengers, the LSV can carry a wide array of armament, including the GAU multi-barrelled .50 MG, the M2 .50 MG, 7.62 mm MGs, the 40 mm M19 grenade-launcher, and Milan anti-tank and Stinger anti-aircraft missiles. The suspension system of the LSV is designed to allow it great mobility over dunes and other rough terrain. The LSV is also designed for very quick turns to allow its weapons to be brought to bear during an ambush.

In a world climate where terrorism is a constant threat, special operations forces are at the forefront of most military operations which often have to be launched quickly and surgically. As a result, developments in special operations weapons and equipment are proceeding at a much more rapid pace than ever before. Today's special operations soldier can eliminate a sentry with a knife but can also eliminate an enemy installation with a laser target-designation system. Whether low-tech or high-tech, the special operator's armoury is constantly being refined and enhanced.

Chapter 4

Airborne and Airmobile Operations

The helicopter has given special operations troops a useful viable alternative to insertions into areas of operation by parachute. Nevertheless, virtually all special operations troops remain airborne-qualified to retain the option of parachute insertion. Initially, special operations troops will receive basic static-line parachute training if they are not already parachute qualified. This training will vary in length in different countries based upon whether they use the parachute training course as a method of selection or whether it is strictly viewed as training in a technical skill. The US basic parachute course lasts three weeks and entails five jumps, while the British course lasts four weeks and includes eight jumps. Upon completion of the basic course, the trainee understands the basics of carrying out jumps, exiting an aircraft properly, correcting parachute problems such as twisted lines or partially collapsed 'chutes, and doing parachute landing falls. He has also joined the 'fraternity of parachutists' which will allow him to carry out jumps with other units with which he may be training or to which he may be temporarily assigned.

Normally, in deciding whether or not to choose airborne insertion for special operations units, certain advantages and disadvantages will have to be considered in relation to a specific mission.

Advantages
- flexibility
- speedy and accurate delivery of personnel, equipment, or supplies
- minimum exposure to hostile counter-measures
- precise navigation to operational area
- ability to deliver supplies and equipment not able to be carried by the individual operators

Parachute insertions in the desert have the advantage of meeting few obstacles, but the parachute will be seen for great distances in the daylight (USNA).

Disadvantages
- vulnerability to enemy air detection and defence systems
- adverse weather conditions
- injury to personnel
- damage or loss of equipment
- need for specially trained aircrews
- need for securing the drop or landing zone

The successful plan for an airborne operation will break into four phases:
- the *mounting phase*, during which the planning, assembling, and marshalling of troops and equipment will take place
- the *air-movement phase* which encompasses events from when the aircraft take off until they deliver troops or supplies to the drop zone
- the *assault phase* which includes the jump and establishment of an airhead
- the *completion of the operation or mission* assigned to those troops inserted via parachute

Operationally, static-line parachute insertions are normally only used when stealth is not necessary and it is desirable to insert a lot of troops quickly. The US Army Rangers specialise in such jumps, particularly to seize airfields or carry out raids in company or battalion strength on high

HALO and HAHO jumps are important insertion methods for special operators. This member of the SAS wears HALO gear.

value enemy installations. The Rangers and many other special operations units learn to do low-level static-line jumps which get them to the ground very quickly so they are exposed to minimal enemy fire. The low-level parachute may be employed at 300 feet and even as low as 250 feet for certain missions. There is also a steerable version of the low-level

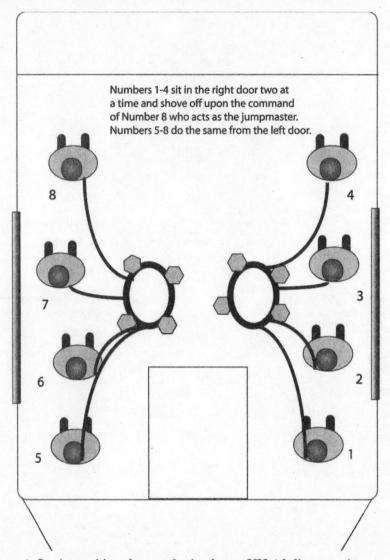

Numbers 1-4 sit in the right door two at a time and shove off upon the command of Number 8 who acts as the jumpmaster. Numbers 5-8 do the same from the left door.

Figure 1 Seating positions for parachuting from a UH-1 helicopter using an expedient anchor system.

parachute, though the low level at which the jumper exits the plane will allow only minimal steering.

Many special operations parachute insertions, however, must be clandestine. As a result, HALO or HAHO insertions are desirable. For HALO insertions, the operators will exit the plane at 20,000 feet or higher, then freefall for about one-and-a-half to two minutes before popping the 'chute at 2,000 to 2,500 feet. At higher altitudes, freefall normally is at about 300 mph, while at lower altitudes it slows to 120 mph in the heavier air. On some HALO operations, jumpers will use an automatic parachute opening mechanism which uses an altimeter to pop the 'chute at a predetermined height. HALO operations allow the aircraft to fly at a height which may cause radar operators to assume it is a commercial flight; hence, they will be less likely to note the HALO jumpers quickly falling off of their screens. SEAL Team Six (Now DevGroup), the US counter-terrorist combat swimmer unit, actually practised jumping from a 727 in case they had to infiltrate via a jump from an airliner. In fact, the ability to carry out HALO operations from commercial airliner altitudes led to an interesting *Soldier* magazine 'April Fools' article some years ago. The article explained with tongue firmly in cheek that the SAS was training for HALO operations from Concorde when it was travelling at Mach 2. US and other special operations forces do practise jumping from bombers, which would allow them to be inserted in enemy controlled territory under the cover of a bombing raid. Of course, another advantage of inserting jumpers from higher altitudes is that it increases the survivability of the aircraft which will be above the range of many SAMs.

Because the HALO jumper exits at higher altitudes, it will be necessary to wear insulated clothing and oxygen. For jumps over 18,000 feet, the operators will have to spend some time pre-breathing one-hundred-per-cent oxygen before exiting the plane. Jumps by US special operations personnel are normally from the ramp of an MC-130. It is so noisy that hand signals are necessary. Normally, the jumpmaster raises his arm to signal 'stand up'. Then, when he extends the arm palm up and touches his helmet, this signals that it is time to move towards the ramp.

When a team is inserted, they can 'fly' using the starfish position and link up in the air by steering themselves towards the team leader who may have a distinctive strobe on his helmet. US MFF trainees practise their technique in a wind tunnel to learn to control their bodies. In fact, the five-week course offered by the US Army Military Freefall Parachute School is a good example of HALO training. In addition to the wind-tunnel training, trainees become fully familiar with the Ram-Air parachute and its deployment procedures as well as learning in-air stability and aerial manoeuvres. During the five weeks, the trainee will make a minimum of 30 freefall jumps, including two day and two night jumps with oxygen and full equipment.

With practice, a jumper can move his arms and legs to steer himself in freefall or can stop a spin by placing the palms hard against the sides as if at attention. In some cases the team will link up in the air at a predetermined height or time. Normally, team members will remain in radio communication, to aid in linkup or in case they need to make any last minute adjustments to the landing point. Usually HALO jumps take place at night with the intention that the operators have little chance of being spotted and can quickly drop off of the radar. During the Cold War, for example, members of the SBS and SAS as well as other NATO special forces practised freefalling into Norwegian fjords, then popping their 'chutes once below radar cover.

In certain terrain, freefall insertions are far more desirable as well. When jumping into mountains, for example, it is advantageous to fall towards valleys or plateaus before deploying the 'chute. With Ram-Air steerable parachutes, the jumper will use toggles to steer the 'chute. Pulling one toggle curls the inside of the canopy down causing the 'chute to rotate, thus allowing turns, while pulling both toggles brakes the 'chute's speed. With US special operations troops, two basic types of 'square mattress' steerable parachutes are in use: the MC-1S and the MT-1B.

Even with skilful jumpers, there is always the chance, however, of drifting towards obstacles which require certain emergency landing procedures. These are three of the most commonly encountered:

- *Wire landing* Although attempts will be made to choose a landing zone (LZ) clear of wires, and the jumper will steer clear if possible, if it does become apparent that a landing in high-tension wires is imminent there are precautions which can be taken. Both feet should be kept together with toes pointed downwards to allow the jumper to slide through the wires. If contact is made with the wires, the jumper should keep his hands high on the inside of the parachute's risers, his chin on his chest, and his body well arched. Rocking by pushing forward on the front risers lessons the chances of becoming entangled.

- *Water landing* Although in certain situations combat swimmers will be inserted via a 'wet jump', normally a water landing can be very dangerous. The substantial number of US and British airborne troops who drowned during the jumps on D-Day can attest to this danger. If the jumper perceives that a water landing is likely, the first step is to pull the saddle of the parachute harness well under the buttocks and sit back in the harness. The headgear should be discarded and the snap connector and restraint strap on the left side of the reserve 'chute should be released. Any equipment attached to the harness that might limit the ability to get out of the harness should be jettisoned. The jumper should grip the opposite main, lift with one hand, and free his leg straps with the other. As soon as contact is made with the water, the jumper should throw his arms upward, arch his body, and slide free of the harness. However, it must be borne in mind that the water may be shallow and a parachute landing fall may still be required.

- *Tree landing* In Malaya, the SAS learned the art of tree-jumping out of necessity, and USAF Pararescue Personnel practise tree landings extensively. However, normally jumpers will attempt to avoid trees. If a landing in trees is necessary, though, the following drills should be followed. The jumper's feet and knees should be placed together and toes pointed downward. Goggles should be pulled down to protect the eyes. Hands should be placed under the opposite armpits with palms facing outward and elbows high. The head should then be rested on the arm to protect the eyes and face, but the jumper should still observe the ground by looking under each elbow. This will help determine is he is going to miss the tree and must prepare for a parachute landing fall.

Another advantage of the combination of freefall and a steerable parachute is that operators may leave from one plane but land precisely at multiple locations to allow simultaneous assaults from different directions.

Freefall parachutists, particularly those acting as jumpmasters, must understand how to calculate the HARP (High-Altitude Release Point). This calculation is based upon a combination of the distance and direction from the desired impact point to the parachute opening pont, the distance and direction from the parachute opening point to the preliminary release point, and compensation for the forward throw. For HAHO missions, forward drift will have to be calculated as well in determining the HARP. Additionally, wind direction in degrees will have to be factored in. Formulas and tables are available to the freefaller to determine his HARP for a HALO or HAHO jump, but today most jumpers have access to systems such as the Garmin Jump Master program which allows relevant information to be punched, then gives the jumper his HARP.

HAHO jumps offer the special operations unit still another option for clandestine insertion. During a HAHO jump, the operators only freefall for eight to ten seconds from 30,000 feet, then deploy their 'chutes. At this altitude, the jumpers can glide twenty-five miles or more to their LZs. In fact, reportedly, well-trained HAHO jumpers have the capability of inserting from even further away using a High-Altitude Parachute-Penetration System (HAPPS). This allows the insertion aircraft to fly out to sea or across an international border yet still insert operators on to their objective. A Ram-Air 'chute has a 3:1 glide ratio, which means it covers three feet forward for every one foot down. By employing a compass, GPS and altimeters, a team can use this glide ratio to their advantage to descend near their objective silently. S-turns will allow them to eat up groundspeed as they approach their landing point. Dark nights are best for HAHO insertions so that the jumpers are not silhouetted against the moon when nearing the ground. Nights with low cloud cover are even better.

Another specialised technique is used to insert combat swimmers such as the SEALs or SBS. Generally known as 'wet jumps', these are para-chute insertions into the ocean off the coast of an objective or near a ship. When carrying out a wet jump, the operator may have a substantial amount of equipment including his weapon, rucksack, ammunition, etc., as well as breathing apparatus, mask, fins, and other swimming gear. During a wet jump it is very important that the operator knows when to jettison his 'chute and to release equipment prior to entering the water. He must also have rigged the equipment for easy recovery after releasing it and then for getting it into an inflatable boat. One of the most critical aspects in determining whether a wet jump may be carried out is the wind speed; the maximum acceptable is about eighteen mph, though choppy seas are not really a major consideration. In general, however, the rule of thumb should be that wet jumps will only be carried out if there is no other possible way to insert the operators for the mission, since they remain quite dangerous. The loss of four SEALs during an unnecessary night jump into the sea with high winds was one of many blunders during 'Operation Urgent Fury', the US invasion of Grenada.

Often in conjunction with a 'wet jump', boats or equipment for SEALs will be delivered via a parachute extraction from an aircraft flying at low level. Known as Low-Level Extraction (LOLEX), this technique is normally used for equipment, but reportedly some combat swimmer units have practised such extractions while strapped into boats. Alternatively, a 'rubber duck' (such as the Zodiac) can be inserted by parachute after it is strapped to a board and the SEALs can parachute and follow it down into the water.

Another type of parachute insertion practised by some special operations units is a 'piggyback' or tandem jump. This technique involves an experienced jumper bringing in another person using a harness rigged for two people. This type of jump would normally only be used when it is necessary to bring in an individual who is key to a mission but who has not had parachute training. For example, if a trained engineer was required for assistance during a sabotage mission or a scientist for a raid on a nuclear, biological, or chemical site, they might piggyback. In a guerrilla warfare scenario, this technique might be used to return an exiled leader to his country.

One innovation which has made it easier for special operations troops to bring high-tech equipment into an area of operations by parachute is the combination of GPS and laser designator which may be used to land a 'chute remotely to carry equipment that an individual parachutist could not bring in.

Normally, it is most cost-effective for a country to have one parachute training school through which personnel from all branches of the armed forces achieve airborne qualification. Reportedly, however, the US Navy SEALs have been considering starting their own parachute school geared more completely to their needs. Trainees would receive their basic static-line training followed by training in HALO, HAHO, and 'wet' jumps. Since SEALs will normally not do standard military static-line jumps, there is a sound argument for having a unified parachute training course more suited to the needs of combat swimmers and which would require less time away at other parachute schools to gain the skills. If, indeed, the SEALs do start their own jump school it would make sense that other units that combine parachuting with swimming such as the US Marine Corps Recons might also choose to send trainees.

According to the US Army Manual (FM 57-38) the Pathfinder is trained to provide 'navigational assistance and air-traffic advisories for Army aircraft encompass(ing) any phase of an air assault or ground operations that require sustained support by Army aircraft.' USAF Combat Controller Teams (CCTs) are trained and equipped to act as ground controllers for USAF aircraft carrying out a wide array of missions. CCTs receive airborne and scuba training as well as other special operations training which allows them to work with other special operators or independently. Both CCTs and Pathfinders are trained to survey drop zones (DZs) for paratroopers or landing zones (LZs) for helicopter-borne troops. At least some special operators receive Pathfinder training to allow them to carry out this mission when working with indigenous troops, particularly for the purposes of calling in aerial resupply. At least some members of Ranger battalions receive Pathfinder training as well since Rangers are trained to jump and seize airfields. Not only can the Pathfinders be first in to survey and mark DZs but they can

USAF Combat Control Team members accompany special ops personnel and act as forward air controllers (USAF).

maintain contact with aircraft during the drop. In some cases both Air Force CCTs and Pathfinders might jump with the Rangers.

Combat Control Teams or special operations Pathfinders will normally infiltrate an area by one of the following means:

- jumping or being delivered by helicopter ahead of other jumpers
- jumping with the first serial of airborne personnel; CCTs assigned to Ranger units will often go in with the lead elements during an assault to seize an airfield
- deploying overland to the objective, normally clandestinely
- insertion by submarine or small boat
- some combination of the previous four (i.e., be inserted from a submarine, swim ashore, then infiltrate overland to the drop area)

Members of the French 2nd Foreign Legion Parachute Regiment rig for a jump (ECP).

Normally, the missions of USAF Combat Control Teams or units in other armed forces with a similar mission include the following requirements:

- to infiltrate or deploy to the the DZ or LZ by the most feasible and expedient means
- to mark the DZ or LZ and/or timing point with appropriate navigational identification aids
- to establish ground-to-air communications
- to establish point-to-point communications with the command

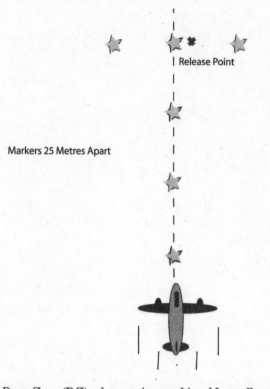

Release Point

Markers 25 Metres Apart

Figure 2   Drop Zone (DZ) release-point marking. Normally, when marking the release point for the parachute drop, six or fewer markers will be used. For operational drops of less than 800 feet, markers will be set 25 metres apart. For drops over 800 feet, the spacing is increased to 50 metres. Markers will be arranged in a shape pre-designated for security, in the illustration a 'T' shape. The drop will be made directly over the last light. When two rows of lights are used, the drop is made directly over the last light in the right-hand row.

structure controlling the troop carriers
- to establish communications with the tactical air-control system
- to relay advice and information to incoming aircraft which may be useful in accomplishing their mission
- to provide weather information which could affect local air operations
- to assist in site selection for LZs or DZs and relay information about them to aircraft in flight
- to act as air-traffic controller for aircraft in the objective area until other ground air-traffic control facilities are in place
- to exercise air-traffic control in the vicinity of the DZ
- if the drop is large enough, to coordinate with unit surgeons on

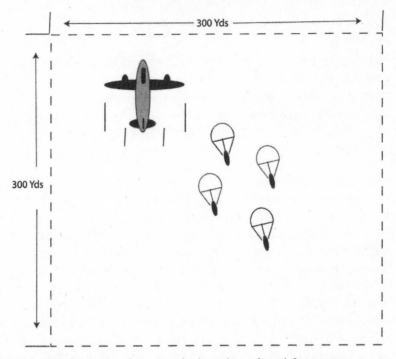

Figure 3 Minimum size drop zone for insertions of special ops teams.

the location of patient staging-points
- to coordinate with unit surgeon or senior combat medic on establishment of MedEvac procedures
- to record any relevant statistical data on the air drop

Although in some cases Pathfinders may have to function in place of CCTs if none are present, they normally have their own mission, which may include providing security for USAF CCTs while they carry out their mission. Among those duties assigned to Pathfinders or special operations personnel trained to function as Pathfinders are the following:

- selection, marking, improvement and control of landing sites
- reconnoitring potential LZs or DZs
- preparing DZs or LZs, which may include setting up visual and electronic navigational aids and removing minor obstacles
- employing ground-to-air radio communications to provide pilots with air-traffic information and useful data
- advising pilots about friendly mortar and artillery fire by maintaining communications with the fire support elements
- providing technical assistance for the assembly of supplies,

equipment, and troops prior to an airborne or airmobile insertion

- offering technical advice and assistance when preparing troops, supplies, or equipment for airborne or airmobile insertion
- providing limited nuclear, biological, and chemical (NBC) monitoring of potential LZs or DZs
- providing limited weather observations, including wind velocity and direction, cloud cover, visibility, and cloud ceiling

In the absence of Air Force CCTs, Pathfinder trained personnel can provide basic ground control for USAF aircraft as well as Army aviation units. Note in regard to the provision of weather information that the USAF has another special unit designated 'Combat Weather' which includes airborne-trained special operators who also receive meteorology training which allows them to parachute into possible areas of operations for more detailed weather assessment. At least some US aircraft used for airborne operations also incorporate technology designed to allow accurate delivery of troops by parachute in adverse weather conditions.

Personnel trained to function as Pathfinders must be capable of operating an array of specialised equipment. Electronic navigation aids including homing beacons, transponders, and radios may all be used to contact aviation elements outside the line of sight. However, visual navigation aids remain important as well; thus, Pathfinders may employ signal panels, smoke, signal mirrors, and coloured gloves during daylight and light beacons, lanterns, baton flashlights, strobe lights, and pyrotechnics at night. Field expedient visual aids may also be used (e.g., a fire burning in the shape of a letter or number). For helicopter pilots equipped with night-vision equipment, infrared navigational aids may be employed. Other electronic equipment may be used to aid troops to assemble upon landing. This may include homing devices or radio signals. Visual assembly aids of the same type as those used as navigational aids may be employed for day or night.

An important aspect of training for all Pathfinders but especially important for special operations personnel functioning as Pathfinders is communications security, since the enemy may be attempting to locate the special operations unit via radio intercept and direction finding or to disrupt an airborne or airmobile operation through disruption of communications. As a result, Pathfinders learn to limit their time on the air and to use succinct code. Fortunately, modern special operations radios are quite secure, but precautions must always be taken to protect the aircraft and personnel being guided in by the Pathfinder.

Because it is very likely that many air operations by special operations units will take place in a high-threat environment, certain Standard Operating Procedures (SOPs) for Pathfinders will be designed with precautions that will ensure mission success. For example, navigation may present a problem for pilots because they will be flying low approaches, often following the terrain. Operations may also be taken into mountainous or other rough terrain. Generally, special operations helicopter pilots are well trained in operations under difficult conditions and at night. However, preplanning by Pathfinders can aid the pilots. For example, two Pathfinders with beacons could be positioned along the approach flight path. For security, the pilots would only turn on the beacon upon receiving a coded message from the pilot that he needs the beacon to check navigation. Pathfinders might also have agreed with the pilot a prearranged code-phrase or word to indicate an immediate threat along the flight path (e.g., enemy with a surface-to-air missile).

If no CCT is available, then Pathfinders can undertake air-traffic control. For the special operator with Pathfinder training, this normally entails bringing in aircraft for resupply or for extraction of casualties. To perform this function, the Pathfinder must understand traffic patterns which can be used to manage the airspace for which he is responsible. Normally, he will employ either a left or right traffic pattern. He must also manage the methods for aircraft to enter the traffic pattern. Once aircraft are in the traffic pattern, then the Pathfinder must ensure that there is proper spacing between aircraft to prevent congestion and accidents. When controlling takeoffs and landings, proper separation between aircraft must be ensured. Normally, coloured lights or smoke may be used for controlling landings and takeoffs (steady green means cleared for takeoff or lift-off or cleared to land, steady red means stop if on the ground or give way to other aircraft and continue circling while in the air). Note that Air Force CCTs will normally carry out most of these functions if they are assigned to a US special operations unit.

For the special operator functioning as a Pathfinder the primary job, however, will most often be to provide his expertise in selecting and assisting in parachute or helicopter landings. When choosing a DZ for either troops or supplies, the Pathfinder must consider a large number of details, including:

- *Air-drop airspeeds* Airspeed determines the time the aircraft will spend over the DZ. The stall speed of the aircraft must be considered as must the type of drop (i.e., static-line or HALO/HAHO).

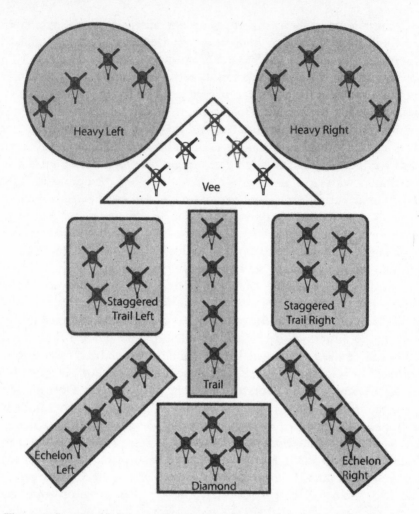

Figure 4 Standard helicopter flight and landing formations.

- *Drop altitude* The Pathfinder must know how to determine drop altitude properly since it is measured from the highest field elevation to the drop aircraft. However, some pilots will be relying on their altimeter which measures their height from sea level. As a result Pathfinders learn to calculate the actual drop altitude by adding the drop altitude required for the operation and the highest field elevation. For example, if the highest field elevation is 650 feet and troops require 800 feet for a tactical static-line drop, then the actual drop altitude will be 1,450 feet. The Pathfinder must also be aware of minimum drop altitudes for heavy equipment, containers, etc.

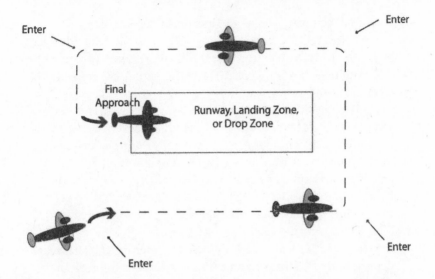

Figure 5 Left traffic pattern. The altitude for the traffic pattern will normally be 1,000 to 1,200 feet above ground level and it may extend out as much as a mile in all directions from the runway, LZ or DZ. As long as it is consistent with safety requirements, aircraft can enter from any direction around the objective as shown. Note that the right-hand traffic pattern will simply be the reverse of the left-hand pattern.

- *Time over DZ estimates* Pathfinders learn the rule of thumb that one second should be allowed for each jumper to exit the door, but the first jumper is not counted. As a result, the time in seconds required will normally be the number of jumpers minus one. For aerial delivery of bundles, three seconds per bundle is required, but the first bundle out the door is not counted in estimating time.
- *Methods of delivery* The Pathfinder must know how to determine whether low velocity, high velocity, or free drop is best for supply drops. One consideration will be how built-up the DZ area is.
- *Obstacles* The Pathfinder attempts to choose a DZ which is free of obstacles or clear obstacles when possible. Special operations personnel who function as Pathfinders may well use their demolition training to clear areas of some DZs. When airborne troops are being delivered, a clear DZ is especially important to prevent injuries. Among the obstacles which should be avoided when selecting a DZ are: trees higher than thirty-five feet, water more than four feet deep within 1,000 metres of the DZ, barbed wire fences, swamps, rocks, ditches or gullies. Great

care must be taken to note the location of power lines.

- *Access* Normally airborne troops will be dropped as near as possible to their objective so care must be taken to choose a DZ which is not separated from the target by impassable terrain.
- *Size* The width of a DZ can be relatively consistent (400 to 450 yards) but length will increase about seventy-five yards with each additional jumper. As a result, multiple passes may be necessary to deliver all personnel. The Pathfinder must also consider wind speed to determine likely drift of equipment.
- *Cover or concealment near the DZ* If there is cover nearby so that troops may quickly move into defensive positions once landed this aids in securing the DZ.
- *Approach and departure routes* When considering approach and departure, the Pathfinder must look at the locations of enemy personnel, especially with SAMs or other anti-aircraft weapons, obstacles to the aircraft such as high-tension wires, terrain which is higher than the DZ, and no-fly areas. The route which allows the DZ to be most readily identifiable from the air is preferable if other factors are equal. A straight approach is also desirable.

Whether trained as Pathfinders or not, special operations personnel will often have to lay out LZs for helicopters and know how to direct in a chopper properly for landing. Although helicopter training is given throughout special operations training, some personnel will also attend a special course. In the US Army, the ten-day Air Assault School is highly respected. Many foreign special operations personnel also attend this school, both as an aid to training their own forces in airmobile tactics and also to equip them better to work with US airmobile troops. During the Air Assault course, personnel learn combat air assault procedures, including the use of the troop ladder, rappelling procedures from towers and helicopters, sling-loading procedures, and aerial medical evacuation procedures.

Although most special operations personnel will not operate in units large enough to carry out a true air assault, some, such as the US Army Rangers or the Royal Marine Commandos, may carry out a company or battalion-sized air assault. Special operations advisors to indigenous troops or foreign military units must also understand the basics of planning and implementing an air assault in case they have to train troops with whom they are working in the techniques.

US Navy SEALs as well as other special operators practise rappelling techniques from helicopters (USNA).

When planning an air assault, five separate plans are required to come together:

- a *Ground Tactical Plan* which specifies what mission those troops carrying out the air assault plan to accomplish and how they will carry out this mission
- a *Landing Plan* which allows the Ground Plan to be implemented by getting the troops to the LZ at the proper time and prepared to carry out their mission
- an *Air-movement Plan* which sets out the schedule and instructions for actually moving troops, equipment, and supplies to the LZ
- a *Loading Plan* which ensures that troops, equipment, and supplies are properly loaded on the correct helicopters so that unit integrity is maintained, command and control may be exerted, and troops are ready to fight upon landing

- a *Staging Plan* which sets out the order that troops, equipment, and supplies arrive at the staging point

When training indigenous troops or taking part in an air assault, the special operator must understand the basics of loading and unloading a helicopter tactically when the helicopter touches down. Normally, tactical unloading when a 'hot' LZ is expected dictates that the door nearest the cover and concealment should be used. Even under fire certain safety drills must be retained. Care must be taken to avoid the rotors and weapons should be kept pointed downward while exiting the chopper.

The special operator functioning as a Pathfinder for airmobile operations must understand the basics of choosing a proper LZ. Among the considerations will be the following:

- *Number of helicopters involved* It will be necessary to determine if the chosen LZ can handle all helicopters necessary for the mission or if they must be landed in successive lifts. In some cases a second LZ may have to be established.
- *Landing formations* Generally, helicopters land in the same formation in which they have been flying; however, when landing in constricted areas it may be necessary to adjust the formation. Formations may also be chosen based on tactical considerations. The 'V' Formation, for example, is best for small LZs and allows rapid deployment of operators to the front. However, it restricts the suppressive fire of inboard door gunners and makes pre-positioning loads difficult. The Echelon Left or Echelon Right Formation requires a relatively long and wide LZ and presents difficulty in pre-positioning loads, but it allows rapid deployment of forces to the flank and allows unrestricted suppressive fire on both flanks, an important consideration in an LZ that may be 'hot'. The Heavy Left or Heavy Right Formation which requires a long, wide LZ presents difficulty in pre-positioning loads, and restricts suppressive fire by inboard gunners, but it does allow suppressive fire to the front and flanks, once again making this a useful formation for a 'hot' LZ. The Diamond Formation allows rapid deployment of troops to provide 360 degree security and requires a smaller LZ, but presents some difficulty in pre-positioning loads and restricts suppressive fire by inboard door gunners. The Trail Formation requires a relatively small LZ and allows rapid deployment of troops to the flanks. It also

Helicopters extracting special operations personnel need to be able to provide their own suppressive fire. Weapons such as this minigun are highly effective (USAF).

simplifies pre-positioning loads and allows unrestricted suppressive fire by the door gunners. The Staggered Trail Left or Staggered Trail Right Formation requires a relatively long, wide LZ, simplifies pre-positioning loads, allows rapid deployment in all directions for all around security of the LZ, but does restrict door gunners' suppressive fire.

- *Surface conditions* LZs must be firm enough so that helicopters will not bog down, and will be free of debris which might be kicked up by the rotors, and, preferably free of sand or snow which can be blown to obscure visibility. Another aspect of the surface of a potential LZ which must be considered is ground slope. Normally, a slope of six per cent or less requires the chopper to land up slope; a slope of seven to fifteen per cent requires the chopper to land side slope; and a slope of over fifteen per cent precludes the chopper touching down and will require the use of a trooper ladder or rope for insertions and a winch for extractions.

- *Approach and departure directions* Helicopters should land over the lowest obstacles and normally into the wind. Departures should also be over the lowest obstacles.
- *Prevailing wind* Normally, the most important consideration is whether there is a crosswind. If it exceeds nine knots this will normally preclude landings.
- *Density altitude* This is determined by a combination of altitude, temperature, and humidity. As the density altitude increases, the size of the LZ must also increase as high, hot, and humid conditions negatively affect helicopter lift capability.
- *Loads* Fully loaded helicopters will need a larger LZ and better approach and departure routes as their ability to ascend or descend vertically will be lowered.
- *Obstacles* LZs should be free of power lines, tall trees, and other obstructions. Within the LZ, smaller obstacles such as rocks, stumps, holes, etc., will also have to be removed. Obstacles which cannot be removed must be clearly marked for day or night landings. Normally, red panels are used to mark rocks, holes, stumps, etc. for day landings and red lights for night landings. Within the actual LZ, the Pathfinder will determine 'Landing Points' which should be level, cleared circular areas between twenty-five and a hundred metres in diameter depending on the type of helicopter. During darkness the chopper will normally need more landing area. For night landings, the landing points may be marked with lights in the shape of a 'Y' or 'T'. Experienced pilots can quickly gauge from the appearance of these letters from the air if they are off course or are approaching with a too shallow or too steep rate of descent. For night landings the inverted 'Y' is usually considered the best option. When multiple helicopters are landing, the inverted 'Y' will normally designate the landing point for the lead aircraft. When multiple helicopters are landing, different-coloured lights may be employed for each landing point to designate who lands where. For security, it is usually a good idea to keep the landing lights turned upside down until helicopters are on final approach. It may be necessary to place filters over the lights if those acting as Pathfinders know the chopper pilots are wearing NVGs as the

German airborne troops quickly move out after a helicopter insertion.

lights may blind them otherwise. Special landing lights designed for NVGs may also be available. Other factors which can affect the size of Landing Point are type of load, climate, and visibility.

When conditions are optimal, the special operator may have time to prepare an LZ, especially if he is working with local indigenous personnel who can help. However, in some circumstances, such as emergency extractions, he will have to determine the best LZ in his area. In cases where troops are being extracted or a medical evacuation is taking place, the helicopter may not even be able to land, and a winch may have to be used while the chopper hovers. Special operators normally make a mental note of any cleared areas near their positions which might allow a helicopter to land in an emergency.

There are other options for extracting special operators as well. For example, the Stabilised Airborne Body Operations (STABO) or Special Procedures Insertion/Extraction (SPIE) rig can be used. The STABO, which is favoured by US Army Special Forces and some other allied units, employs individual ropes with harnesses which are lowered for each operator, though a safety rope normally links them together. The SPIE uses a single rope with multiple harnesses and is favoured by the US Navy SEALs. With either rig, the helicopter will actually extract the operators while they are hanging from the rig and winch them in while leaving the area. Helicopter pilots who work with the US Navy SEALs have also practised an extraction technique in which they hover just above the water with the rear ramp of the helicopter actually open and water flooding the floor of the chopper. SEALs then pilot their rubber boats directly into the helicopter for extraction.

When acting as a Pathfinder for helicopter ops, the special operator will normally determine alternative LZs as well in case tactical conditions change or other events require a move.

As helicopters approach an LZ, there will normally be a Communications Checkpoint (CCP) where the Controller/Pathfinder gives the flight leader or helicopter pilot the heading from the CCP to the LZ. Other information which might be given during the communications check includes:

- enemy situation
- friendly fire
- LZ elevation
- landing formation
- terrain conditions
- air-traffic situation
- obstacles on the LZ
- marking of LZ with smoke, lights, panels, strobes, etc.
- visual approach path indicator settings
- next reporting point

To aid aircraft en route to an LZ, Pathfinders will install electronic and visual navigation aids if the aids are available. They will also make contact using ground-to-air radio if they have a set. Pathfinders should also organise LZ security if they have enough troops available.

Some special considerations will be in effect for LZs in mountains, deserts, jungle, snow, or other terrain. However, specialised drills will be discussed in chapters dealing with these areas of operations.

Airborne or airmobile insertions remain extremely important methods for getting special operators into their area of operations. As a result, special operations units will include parachute or helicopter operations as an integral part of their training and will normally have certain personnel,

Special ops personnel learn extraction techniques for when the helicopter cannot land. In this case, personnel are from ESI, the Belgian counterterrorist unit (FIRE).

as in the SAS HALO Troops or the US Army Special Forces HALO Detachments, who keep up with the latest developments in military free fall parachuting so that they can report on these innovations to their comrades and also help develop doctrine for operations by their units.

Chapter 5

Amphibious, Combat-Swimmer, and Small-Boat Ops

N aval or Marine special warfare units normally have a wide array of missions related to their ability to operate on, under, or near the water. Typical missions may include:

- *Maritime counter-terrorism* This can include hostage rescue aboard cruise ships or liners, private yachts, ferries, or other craft. Interdiction of ships carrying WMDs or terrorists is normally included as well.
- *Protection of oil platforms* Many countries maintain off-shore oil platforms in the North Sea, Gulf of Mexico, Persian Gulf or elsewhere. Special warfare units normally have a dual role of protecting these rigs from attack or retaking them if they are seized by terrorists.
- *Support of law-enforcement agencies or military units in drug suppression or other smuggling operations* Owing to their specialised skills in clandestinely boarding ships at sea, special operations units may be asked to assist other agencies in certain operations against organised crime, especially since many terrorists fund their operations through drug smuggling. Interdicting illegal aliens who may actually be terrorists may also involve special operations units.
- *Beach reconnaissance and hydrographic surveying* Combat swimmers and small boat units retain the mission of surveying beaches prior to amphibious operations. These missions may also include clearance of underwater obstacles.
- *Recovery of sensitive or classified equipment from under water* In some cases, items with intelligence value may have been lost and will require combat swimmers or divers to recover them.
- *Amphibious diversion operations* Small numbers of amphibious

commandos or combat swimmers may be sent to create diversions along coastlines to convince an enemy that a landing is taking place. Diversion operations will normally be intended to pull troops away from the actual point of attack.

• *Rescue of downed airmen near the water* Naval or other pilots who have gone down on islands or near the coast may be rescued by special operations personnel who infiltrate under water or by small boat. A standard technique used by some special operations units is to send in a scout swimmer or a pair of scout swimmers to make initial contact with the downed airman, then call in additional personnel and rescue boats.

• *Reconnaissance of enemy installations near the coast and possibly target designation for attacks against these installations* Just as other special operations forces may infiltrate near an installation to gather intelligence or use target designators to guide in 'smart' munitions, naval special warfare personnel will carry out these same missions against harbours, naval installations, etc. The US Navy specifically sends some SEALs for training in the use of laser target designators. Their tactics include infiltration from the sea to 'paint' facilities close to the water. Although only contemplated for use during the Cold War, US Navy SEALs were trained and equipped to carry out missions using Special Atomic Demolition Munitions (SADM).

• *Raids along enemy coastlines* Naval special warfare personnel can infiltrate to carry out raids against enemy installations, to assassinate key personnel, or to snatch enemy personnel for interrogation.

• *Maritime and riverine counter-insurgency* Naval special warfare forces may be used in counter-insurgency operations to interdict guerrilla supply routes along waterways or from the sea. Operators may also launch raids or ambushes against guerrilla forces with camps or infiltration routes along waterways.

Beach reconnaissance and clearance was the original mission of forerunners of today's SEALs and SBS as well as other units. Although not as glamorous as some other missions, scouting beaches for amphibious landings remains an important element of current naval special ops. In the US Navy, there were originally Underwater Demolition Teams (UDTs) who had the mission of beach clearance, while the SEALs retained the special warfare mission. However, the UDTs were combined with the SEALs some years ago and the SEALs now train for both missions. In fact, there is normally a SEAL Amphibious Ready Group (ARG) assigned to each US Marine Expeditionary Unit specifically to carry out hydrographic reconnaissance if needed.

Normally beach survey and clearance missions will be carried out in three primary phases:

- The beach reconnaissance unit will be assigned beaches to survey for possible landings. The teams will generally be inserted at night by fast boats a few hundred metres offshore, then will swim in to the beach. Once near the beach, the hydrographic survey will be carried out. Team members will chart the depth of water with a lead line, and chart locations of reefs, rocks, or other underwater obstacles. GPS systems may be used to aid in accurate charting. As the teams check the approaches to the beach, they will make notes on the most likely lanes of approach for amphibious landings. In addition to charting offshore approaches, team members will also chart beach defences.

    The cast and recovery system, in which a rubber boat is attached to a speedboat, allowing SEALs to roll into the rubber boat, then into the sea, will often be used for insertions. After the survey, recovery will be carried out in reverse. Combat swimmers reach the rendezvous point, then kick their flippers to raise themselves as high as possible in the water. As the boat approaches, the swimmer raises his arm which is snagged by a rubber ring. Recoveries can be made at speeds up to thirteen knots.
- Once the beach survey is completed, the survey team will exfiltrate from the beach, be picked up, and return to their command element. After assembling their data in usable form, they will present it to the officer in charge of the amphibious forces.
- Once the surveys have been studied by the commander of any landing forces, the combat swimmers may be sent back to clear approaches with satchel charges and detonating cord.

Often in training combat swimmers will survey beaches which may one day become possible landing sites. As a result, any surveys should be retained for future reference. During the Falklands War, for example, some beaches had already been surveyed by members of the Royal Marines who had been stationed there. US Navy SEALs frequently compile information on beaches in South Korea, Taiwan, the Philippines, and other areas where they help train indigenous personnel. Although the surveys may be carried out as part of training operations with local combat swimmers, if US amphibious landings ever prove necessary, it can prove invaluable. On the other hand, there is no way to predict where an amphibious landing might be required. US forces had not anticipated the need for an amphibious landing on the island of Grenada; hence, SEALs had to carry out a beach reconnaissance prior to USMC landings.

During the Gulf War, US Navy SEALs had been assigned to carry out hydrographic reconnaissance of possible landing sites. However, instead of actually carrying out the landings, the SEALs were sent back to create a diversion during the invasion of Kuwait and Iraq. SEALs planted explosives along the beaches and sped back and forth in fast boats firing at the shore. Reportedly, two Iraqi divisions were tied down in anticipation of a US Marine landing.

When infiltrating a beach, either for a reconnaissance mission or a raid, combat swimmers may swim on the surface with their faces blackened and their mask down on their necks to prevent reflection. Normally, they will only go under water when nearing the objective. This technique is especially useful for harbour infiltrations when explosive devices may be planted on enemy ships.

US Navy SEALs are often inserted from small boats (USNA).

In deciding whether or not infiltration from the water is viable for a certain mission, the advantages and disadvantages must be considered as follows:

Advantages

- Delivery capability over long ranges
- Relative freedom from weather considerations prior to embarkation
- En route operational briefings, rehearsals, and intelligence updates are possible
- Large quantities of supplies and equipment may be transported via surface craft

Disadvantages

- Time required for unloading and trans-shipment from off-shore drop-off points
- Vulnerability of landing operations to hostile shore-defence
- Loss of personnel during ship-to-ship movement
- Limited cargo capacity when inserted from submarines
- Need for special training
- Need to waterproof equipment
- Effects of sea and surf conditions caused by high winds. For some raiding missions or beach reconnaissances, canoes offer a better method of infiltration. Canoes have the advantage of maintaining a low profile, being virtually noiseless, and having no mechanical propulsion systems to fail. The two-man Klepper canoe is still widely used by the SAS and SBS as well as dozens of other special operations units. Currently, the SBS uses the Klepper Aerius II, which employs a wooden frame and canvas and rubber skin. It can be broken down into three bags for ease of transport. Generally, one operator carries the skin, anchor, and compass, while the other carries the wooden frame and paddles.

Whether launched in canoes, rubber boats, swimmer delivery vehicles, or as swimmers, naval special operators will often be delivered near to their objective by submarine. The procedure is fairly similar in most combat swimmer units. The submarine will take the swimmers within a mile or two of shore at night. A couple of divers then enter the escape chamber. Once it has been sealed and filled with water, they exit the submarine, inflate a buoy, and send it to the surface. Then they inflate a rubber boat and attach it to the buoy. Once everything is prepared, the rest of the team dons diving gear and locks out of the submarine and swims up to the boat, a Combat Rubber Raiding Craft (CRRC) or similar 'rubber duck'. If these rubber craft have a motor, it is designed to be very quiet for infiltration missions. Canoes or small boats can also be towed by the submarine which rides at periscope depth.

It is not in the scope of this work to cover actual scuba techniques in detail, but a few comments should be made about the closed-circuit systems most likely to be used by combat swimmers for missions. The Closed-Circuit Oxygen Rebreather retains exhaled breath without releasing bubbles by carrying the exhaled gas to a carbon dioxide scrubber which removes the carbon dioxide and returns the clean gas for reuse. The Closed-Circuit Mixed Gas System allows deeper dives without bubbles and reduces danger of oxygen poisoning. Combat swimmer units spend a substantial amount of time learning the symptoms of oxygen poisoning and steps to be taken if these symptoms are noticed. US Navy SEALs, for example, learn to use the acronym VENTID to remember likely symptoms as follows:

V   Vision blurred or tunnel
E   Ears ringing
N   Nausea
T   Twitching, usually facial
I   Irritability
D   Dizziness

In harbour raids or other operations which will be carried out by combat swimmers, the 'frogmen' normally operate in swimming pairs so they can watch out for each other. Underwater navigation skills are extremely important to allow the swimmers to find their objective in the darkness and/or under water. Experienced combat swimmers learn to use the currents in a harbour to their advantage. This allows them to drift towards their objective without creating traces in the water. If multiple objectives are to be attacked, the one which will allow them to drift towards the second one will be approached first. If only one is to be attacked, the swimmers will approach with the drift and let it carry them to the objective. Among other techniques which have proven useful is the SBS method of using a buoyancy bag to carry explosives or weapons while swimming. This bag is partially filled with water which renders it weightless when partially submerged. For harbour or beach infiltrations, this allows greater weight to be transported without unduly tiring the

Demolition skills are invaluable to special ops personnel as with this Royal Marine Commando helping to clear mines in the Falklands (IWM).

swimmers. At least some combat swimmer units have experimented with body-armour carriers that also act as flotation devices. However, since getting Kevlar wet normally degrades its ability to stop bullets, there are obvious disadvantages to this combination.

When combat swimmers are planning a beach or harbour infiltration, various factors must be taken into consideration including:

- time limits imposed by breathing apparatus

- distance to be covered underwater
- water temperature and weather affecting the state of the sea
- boat traffic in the area
- lighting in the area as well as shadow and shade
- noise from ships, machinery, dry-dock workers, etc. which can cover sounds created during the approach
- cover provided by docks, bridges, ships, etc.
- sentries and whether they have NVGs
- any blind spots shielded from sentries
- any possible diversions which can be used to cover the operation

While actually swimming, operators must take care to avoid fast surface swimming, splashing on the surface, movement that creates ripples or waves, breaking the surface when diving, creating bubbles in calm open water, multiple swimmers bunching up, creating a silhouette when leaving the water, allowing reflections or lights to be seen, and leaving tracks or equipment on the beach. It is important, too, that at least one or two team members scout ahead to identify trip wires, mines, sentries, or other dangers on a beach.

Combat swimmers may also be launched from submarines using some type of swimmer delivery vehicle (SDV). At least some US submarines which have been equipped to support the SEALs have a Dry-Deck Shelter (DDS) on the outer hull for transporting an SDV. The shelter is connected to the sub's interior by a watertight hatch. Within the DDS, however, is everything needed by combat swimmers for launching their missions and returning, including a decompression chamber. An entire sixteen-man SEAL platoon and its equipment may be carried in the DDS. Since this platoon is the largest SEAL contingent normally assigned an underwater mission, the DDS's capacity meets the requirements for virtually all missions. However, to launch an SDV the entire DDS must be flooded. Surface SEAL craft may also be launched from the DDS. The later Advanced SEAL Delivery Vehicle (ASDV) is designed to piggyback directly onto the submarine and eliminate the need for the DDS.

In some cases, SDVs or small boats may be used in conjunction with helicopters for maritime special operations. When boarding ships at sea, for example, the two may be used in conjunction. Small boats approach the ship at high speed from the rear. It is important that teams assigned to carry out such missions have practised so that they are aware of the proper approach angle and thus are not seen by those aboard the ship. Once the small boat has slipped close to the moving vessel, a telescoping

Combat swimmers may be inserted directly into the sea offshore (USNA).

pole or ladder with hooks is affixed to the ship and operators climb towards the deck. They need to have mastered the skill of shooting an enemy with a suppressed weapon while climbing in case they are spotted by a sentry who peers over the side of the ship. Normally, a few operators will climb aboard and secure the immediate area and possibly move out to secure the bridge. Usually, however, to get more operators on deck quickly a helicopter will approach from the rear after flying just above the waves. When just behind the ship, the helicopter will quickly gain altitude and insert additional personnel via fast rope. It is extremely important, though, that the pilots have practised this manoeuvre in varied conditions since they will constantly have to adjust their height to match the rise and fall of the target vessel. Snipers trained to shoot from helicopters may offer support during the boarding and be prepared to eliminate any enemy fighters attempting to engage the boarding teams. Other members of the special operations team may have been gathering intelligence about the ship and its occupants by posing as fishermen or pleasure-boat operators in close proximity.

Since an assault is easier when a ship is not moving, it is much easier to attack it in port. During the *Achille Lauro* hijacking, in fact, SEAL Team Six, the US naval counter-terrorist unit, had plans to approach the cruise ship using an SDV, then foul the ship's screws with chains so it would not be able to get under way.

However SEAL Team Six, now renamed DevGroup, has also practised assaults at sea extensively. One scenario assumes an ocean liner has been hijacked and a sixteen-man SEAL platoon tasked with assaulting it. Using this plan, SEALs would jump into the sea using steerable parachutes. Rubber boats would be dropped with them using techniques already discussed in the chapter on airborne operations. The drop would normally be about fifty miles away from the liner. Once the distance to the ship has been covered, the rubber boats would coordinate speed with the ship so that extendable poles or ladders may be used, as has previously been mentioned. Some operators have also practised scaling the sides of ships using magnets on hands and feet, but this technique is very slow. One of the greatest difficulties in assaulting a ship is the sheer area which must be covered since ships are by nature broken into a great many interior spaces. As a result, a decision must be made about the most critical areas (e.g., the bridge, points where hostages are held, the engineering space, etc.) and these must be secured first. It may be necessary, too, to establish a holding area where hostages can be separated from hijackers.

As they are so familiar with methods for assaulting ships, special operations personnel may be assigned to protect ships against terrorists or pirates. This will include security in port as well as at sea. Special operators, for example, can advise ship's personnel on security details, security lighting, and techniques such as incorporating 'rat guards' on mooring lines to make them difficult to scale. Both in port and at sea, patrols with shotguns can discourage attack and can also repel boarders with a deadly hail of buckshot. Marksmen armed with select-fire rifles and night optics can be positioned on higher points overlooking the deck areas to give supporting fire against boarders. NVGs should be available for operators assigned to keep a ship secure for use at sea and in port. At sea especially, flares should be available so anyone attempting to board can be illuminated and attacked.

Special operations personnel doing ship's security will have to practise clearing drills designed for use in ships' passageways and compartments. Many of the same tactics used in hostage rescue will apply, including the use of stun grenades if ship's personnel are being held. However, fire and movement drills will have to be adjusted for a ship's configuration, including movement around corners, through watertight doors, etc. Special frangible ammunition may be necessary because many ships have a lot of steel which can cause ricochet. Fortunately, naval special warfare personnel who practise assaulting ships will learn a great deal about defending them in the process. Nevertheless, they will have to rehearse drills for defending as well as attacking if assigned to maritime counter-terrorist or counter-piracy operations.

One of the most difficult maritime counter-terrorist or raiding missions

Special operators must be able to move along jungle waterways. In this case Contra rebels trained by US personnel use locally made boats.

is against oil rigs. Although a static objective, oil rigs present an array of specialised problems for assault units. The US DevGroup, British SBS, German GSG-9, and Australian SAS TAG among others rehearse operations against oil rigs and share lessons learned. Although any oil-rig assault is difficult, missions involving those rigs in the North Sea are especially difficult because of the weather that is likely to be encountered.

Because terrorists or defenders of an oil rig will have the advantage of height which allows them to monitor approaches, an assault will most likely take place at night. An alternative in attacking an enemy-controlled oil rig is to send a gunboat to fire on it before an assault to force any defenders inside. When Iranians were using oil rigs in the Persian Gulf to launch attacks against shipping, this tactic was practised by US SEALs. Once defenders have been driven indoors, helicopters can then insert an assault team via fast rope. Most scenarios involving oil rigs, however, contemplate having to retake an oil rig which has been occupied by terrorists or, as in Iraq recently, seizing a rig before it can be destroyed.

For these missions, a stealthy approach is desirable. Normally, the initial assault element will infiltrate under water or by small boat, then send a couple of men to 'free climb' (i.e., without ropes) up the legs of the rigs. Once these 'scouts' are in position, they can hook up ladders and drop them for the next wave, while maintaining a watch for defenders. In seas that are at all choppy, members of the assault team may actually have to wait for a wave to lift them into position to grab the ladder. If the assault team has swum into position, as soon as an operator is on the ladder he will remove his fins and attach them to his belt. Once the ascent of the ladder begins, it may take an hour or more to reach the platform, especially in heavy seas. Four to five man teams will usually operate together. One member of each team sill normally be armed with a suppressed SMG such as the Heckler & Koch MP5 SD for elimination of sentries.

Once teams are in position, they will usually ascend to high points on the platform where they can control it with fields of fire. In a hostage situation, if the location of the hostages is known, they may move immediately into position for rescue. However, because of the size of an oil platform, many assault plans call for additional personnel to follow up this initial assault element by fast-roping on to the platform. The teams which were inserted from the sea will cover the helicopters and additional personnel. Once the exterior of the platform is controlled and sufficient personnel are available, interior spaces will be cleared.

Use of the helicopter may also be combined with the insertion of combat swimmers for certain types of operations. Known as 'helo-casting', this technique employs a helicopter from which swimmers jump directly into the sea. This technique is widely practised by units such as the SBS, SEALs, and USMC Recons. Generally, it is considered safest if the rule of 10/10 is followed which indicates that swimmers should be inserted at a height of 10 feet at a speed of 10 knots. However, highly trained combat swimmers have practised such insertions at 40/40 or 40 feet and 40 knots. To recover swimmers from the water, the helicopter crew will lower ladders for the swimmers to grab.

During the 'War against Terrorism', naval special operations forces have been used against ships at sea to search for terrorists or WMDs. US Navy SEALs practise what they term Visit, Board, Search, and Seizure (VBSS) operations.

Some waterborne operations take place on rivers rather than the ocean. This is especially true during counter-insurgency operations when interdiction of resupply to guerrillas via waterways is a primary mission. Brazil's GRUMEC unit, for example, does extensive training for counter-insurgency operations along the Amazon. Units such as the US Army Rangers or British Royal Marine Commandos as well as other special operations units may carry out raids across lakes or rivers and will employ techniques which they have rehearsed extensively. For example, raiding forces may have to use improvised bridges to cross rivers. A single rope bridge is the easiest method for river crossing. Once a crossing point is chosen, security is established up- and downstream, and a couple of strong swimmers are sent across to reconnoitre the opposite bank and

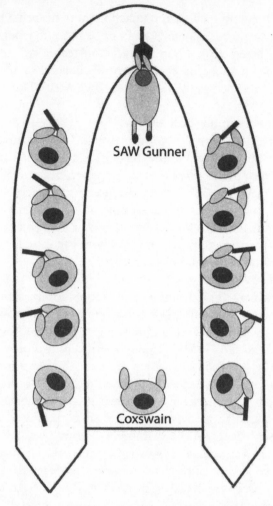

Figure 6 Deployment on a small boat. If a Special Forces A Detachment of twelve men is being carried along with a coxswain, then an additional operator will have to fit in. Otherwise the team leader will function as a coxwain and the boat will stay with the team. On many missions the coxswain and possibly the bow light machine-gunner will stay with the boat.

establish an anchor point. An anchor point is also established on the side from which the crossing will be launched. Operators should be familiar with techniques for traversing a rope bridge, including the commando crawl (on top of the rope with one foot hooked on the rope), the monkey crawl (hanging below the rope with heels crossed over it), and the rappel seat (with a harness or rope rappel seat clipped to the rope with a karabiner). Lifeguards who are good swimmers are established on each

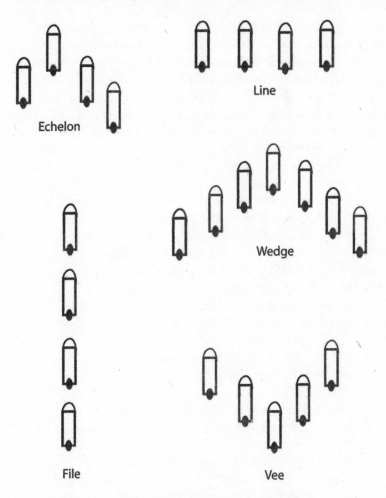

Figure 7 Small boat formations for control, speed and security.

side in case any personnel need to be rescued during the crossing. Normally, for security no more than three team members will be on the rope bridge at any given time, one being unhooked on the far bank, one in the centre, and one hooking up to begin crossing.

US Army Rangers and other special operators learn to use a poncho raft to cross rivers or streams as well. Generally, this method will only be used if the current is not swift and when the river is too wide to use a rope bridge. Once a crossing point has been chosen, personnel pair off and construct the poncho raft with their weapons and equipment inside the two ponchos. With practice, special operations personnel can construct these rafts quite quickly and efficiently. However, since the weapons will

115

be transported inside the poncho raft, it is important that sufficient team or unit members are left on security duty during the crossing and that those who have already crossed can quickly get their boots back on and their weapons ready to provide security for those who will begin crossing.

Assault boats will also be used for raids by Special Forces, Rangers, or Commandos as well as by amphibious special operations personnel. The Zodiac inflatable boat is typical of those used for raids. Normally, this type of boat will carry ten operators as well as a coxswain. Each of the five operators who ride on each side will be assigned an area to observe. The coxswain will be in charge of the boat and will operate the engine if there is one. He maintains the course and sets the boat's speed. If the boat is rowed, the second man on each side sets the pace. One advantage of inflatable boats such as the Zodiac is that the crew may carry them overland when necessary to move towards the water. If the landing will be carried out against an unsecured site, then some scout swimmers may be sent ashore ahead of the landing. Or, if multiple boats are being used for the assault, one boat can land and secure the landing site. Usually the security perimeter will be established fifteen to twenty-five metres inland from the landing point.

During river movement, it is important to take into consideration the characteristics of the river including:

- bends which might hide an enemy ambush
- sloughs (dead-end branches, normally identifiable by lack of current)
- dead water which might contain snags and debris
- an island, upstream portions of which should be approached with care as they tend to accumulate debris
- narrows which will usually have stronger currents
- curves which will usually have faster current on the outside of the curve and sandbars and shallow water on the inside
- overhanging vegetation and projections from the bank (in the jungle snakes may be in overhanging branches)

Depending upon the tactical situation, whether it is day or night, and the width and currents in the river, the team leader will choose the formation when multiple boats are used. The formations usually chosen are the wedge, the line, the file, the echelon or the vee. The line is usually best for landing as it brings the maximum number of weapons into position rapidly in case the landing is contested.

Chapter 6

Operating in All Types of Terrain

Here we shall consider the three major categories of terrain: desert, arctic and mountain, and jungle.

Desert

Desert operations require the devotion of a substantial portion of the special operators' energy to the basics of surviving. Dehydration, sunstroke, and sunburn add to the difficulty of desert operations. The extremes of temperature sap energy and make even simple tasks seem difficult. Not only is water difficult to find, but the heat may cause operators to drink up to three gallons of water a day. Although special operations personnel learn survival techniques such as the construction of solar stills, they still must carry large amounts of water. The loss of salt in perspiration requires either the use of salt tablets or extra salt on food to replace it. As bad as the heat is during the day, the cold can be overwhelming at night. SAS patrols operating in Iraq during the Gulf War found that their clothing was too light for the bitter cold they encountered. It must be borne in mind that in some deserts temperatures may fluctuate by up to seventy degrees between night and day. In some desert areas, flash floods can present a danger if the rains suddenly come, and operators must know to head immediately for high ground. Wadis especially must be used with great care as they often offer the easiest routes in the desert and are useful for concealment but can be quickly inundated with water, even if rains have not occurred in the immediate area.

Although water discipline is critical for desert ops, personal hygiene cannot be neglected, since disease, rashes, or other medical problems can incapacitate operators. Lice, mites, and fleas not only cause discomfort but also carry diseases such as dysentery and scrub typhus. In addition to body hygiene, it is important to clean cooking utensils and to dispose of

The roots of the SAS desert skills can be traced to David Stirling and the wartime SAS (IWM).

human waste and garbage carefully. Care of the feet is important, especially as overheating in leather boots can cause problems. Specially designed desert boots such as those from Danner discussed earlier are ideal, and preferable to standard issue. Operators must also be aware of snakes which seek warmth at night and may crawl into a sleeping bag in the cold desert nights. Spiders and scorpions are another danger: they often find boots inviting.

Special care must be taken to maintain weapons and equipment in the desert. Covering weapons when not in use can help to keep sand out of the actions; excess oil should be removed to make sand less likely to stick, and plastic wrap or condoms may be used to cover muzzles. Desert vehicles for special operations teams are normally quite heavily armed with machine-guns and grenade- or rocket-launchers. These give the patrols a great deal of firepower for hit-and-run raids, but the weapons systems must be protected from sand and dust. Radios must also be protected and maintained. Desert heat, for example, can cause solder to become brittle, thus loosening connections. Batteries will have to be recharged more frequently in the desert as well.

Vehicles which are used in the desert may have to be specially designed or modified for such operations. SAS Land Rovers, for example, have enhanced cooling systems, carry channels to allow movement over soft sand, are equipped with winches, have extra fuel tanks, have smoke grenade dischargers installed to help cover a retreat, and may incorporate various other features as well. Maintenance is very important to prevent breakdowns far from assistance. Units such as the SAS Mobility Troops, in fact, expect operators to be able to perform virtually any maintenance or repair on their vehicles. Operators learn special techniques to allow their vehicles to operate more effectively in the desert. For example, a team member will often debus and climb a dune on foot to make sure the vehicle will not get stuck in soft sand or to check the steepness of the slope. When moving through soft sand, tyres will often be partially deflated to offer a wider footprint to gain traction; however, some type of compressor must be carried so the tyres can be reinflated once out of the soft sand. Special sand tyres are also available and are usually mounted on SAS Mobility Troop vehicles.

Because of the difficulty of concealment in the desert as well as the heat, movement will normally be at night with the operators lying up during the daytime to rest and avoid compromise. Heat exhaustion or other related disorders must be avoided and care must be taken even when resting. Lying directly on the sand, for example, exposes an operator to temperatures thirty to forty-five degrees hotter than the air. Digging a shallow trench not only reveals cooler sand upon which to rest but also offers a bit more concealment. Staying concealed in the desert is especially difficult due to the lack of overhead cover, the increased range at which movement can be distinguished, the ease of spotting tracks, especially from the air, and the bright tones of desert sands which will draw attention to anyone or anything not well-camouflaged. In fact, total concealment is difficult to achieve but with care operators and their equipment can be effectively camouflaged. Making concealment as well as detection of an enemy even more difficult is the fact that visibility can change from thirty miles to thirty feet within a matter of minutes in the desert if a sandstorm blows up, and when the storm abates a position may have been revealed by the effects of drifting sand.

Since special operations personnel normally use some type of all-terrain vehicle for desert ops, operators must be aware that vehicle movement will produce dust, exhaust, especially from diesels, and obvious tracks. Moving slowly can lower the dust signature, but it also leaves teams exposed longer. Care must also be taken to avoid reflection from rifle scopes, windshields, or vehicle windows. Normally, rifle optics should be kept covered and windshields lowered if possible. Vehicle silhouettes are also a problem, but removing tops helps lower the silhouette. Camouflage paint and local dirt or sand on the vehicle can help camouflage it as well. Normally, special desert camouflage nets should be carried for covering the vehicles when stopped during the day. It is also a good idea to carry poles to raise the netting away from the vehicles to disguise their shape, but poles should not give the appearance of a tent. Currently, camouflage covers which help screen infrared are used to help screen lay-up points in the cooler evenings. Different sizes can make a shape appear more natural. Cutting some desert scrub to insert around the camouflage net can help hide it even more. Vehicle tracks should be obliterated within fifty metres of where the vehicles are hidden. If the camouflaged vehicle can be sited in shadow or vegetation that is even better. One of the most common ways vehicles are identified in the desert is by morning or evening shadows, so if possible a vehicle hide should be placed in total shadow, which is generally difficult to find in the desert. If this is not possible, placing the vehicle so that the maximum vertical area faces the sun will normally result in the most minimal shadow possible. Digging the vehicle in also reduces the area exposed to cast a shadow. If there are a lot of pebbles near the site, it is better to avoid driving over them since when they are pressed into the ground the tracks are more visible from the air. Finally, it is important to remember that, while the vehicle should be well-camouflaged, it must nevertheless remain ready for a quick departure if necessary.

Navigation in the desert can be quite difficult due to the lack of landmarks. Although many special operators still know how to find their position from the stars, most now rely on the GPS to determine their location or to call in air strikes against targets they might locate. Since much of the driving will be done at night NVGs are critical as well.

US Special Forces often operate in the desert using what they term the Desert Mobility Vehicular System, which comprises two off-road motorcycles, two HMMWVs with weapons systems mounted, and two HMMWVs with attached trailers to carry extra fuel, water, etc. A twelve-man ODA can operate in the desert for extended operations using this

For mobility, members of the French 2nd REP often air transport their vehicles when deployed (ECP).

system. The motorcycles are a key element since they can be used to scout ahead and help navigate. The motorcycle riders use NVGs but often find soft sand or other areas where the 'Humvees' would have trouble by taking a tumble!

Since there are generally only a few routes that can be used to cross desert areas, it is relatively easy to determine enemy movement by observation; however, possible escape routes are fewer and movement by special operations personnel is somewhat constrained. Crossroads are especially important in the desert since traffic from all directions will converge at a few critical points. A great deal can be learned about enemy intentions if observation posts can be established near crossroads. A traditional role of special operations personnel in the desert dating back to the founding of the SAS is carrying out raids against an enemy's lines of communication, which are normally elongated in the desert. An oasis may offer an appealing point for water resupply and a useful point to observe enemy troops, but it must be considered that an oasis in the Sahara may well be one of the most heavily populated and frequently visited places on earth in relation to its size.

When it is necessary to replenish water, there are some basic rules which may help. For example, limestone is easily dissolved by water; therefore, caverns are often etched into it by groundwater. Such caverns are likely to contain springs. Lava rock is another good source for seeping groundwater as it is porous. Valleys that cross the lava flow will often have streams along the walls. If a canyon cuts through a layer of porous sandstone there may also be water seepage. Another technique is to look for animal trails leading to water or to watch for certain birds such as parrots or pigeons which must live near to water. Certain plants will also indicate the presence of water, such as cattails, greasewoods, willows, elderberry, rushes, and salt grass: all of these grow only where there is groundwater near the surface. Normally, if an operator digs near these plants he will find water. Various plants contain water, too, and may be tapped for it.

One of the most important aspects of desert warfare for special operators is acclimatisation. Approximately two weeks are needed to fully acclimatise so if a unit can deploy to a desert environment a couple of weeks ahead of insertion into the area of operations, they will be much more effective. Units with frequent desert commitments such as SAS Mobility Troops spend as much time in the desert as possible to shorten the re-acclimatisation process. Experience will also teach operators the need for high-quality sunglasses or goggles. Eyelids will also be cleaned daily to remove sand which can cause various eye problems. Experienced desert operators will normally use some type of scarf or bandanna to protect the head and face. In fact, typical Arab headdress is often adopted, both for function and to help conceal the identities and nationalities of those wearing it. One of the most important lessons to learn for desert deployment is to drink more water than the operator might think he needs since thirst may not always be the best warning of dehydration. Still another advantage of extensive desert training is that units learn the effects of optical path bending which can make a target appear lower or higher than it really is or nearer or further away. Observing from an elevated point will help minimise optical path bending.

Arctic and mountain

Surprisingly, many of the problems accompanying operations in the snow-covered north are quite similar to those encountered in the desert: health concerns, mobility, water supply, and concealment among others. It will come as a surprise to many that water supply can be a problem in a vast area of snow and ice, but often the amount of fuel necessary to melt snow or ice on stoves creates logistic difficulties. Snow is an inefficient source of water in another way as well since seventeen cubic inches of loose snow yields only one cubic inch of water. A far better source of water is from beneath river or lake ice. Water is usually clearer on the leeward side where there is usually less drifting snow. Ice may be so thick, however, that shaped explosive charges are necessary to create a waterhole. Water will still have to be treated with purification tabs, too. To avoid some possible health problems, if possible personnel should not be selected for arctic missions who have circulatory problems affecting the extremities, skin grafts on the face, inner ear difficulties, or a previous history of severe cold injury. Generally, the rigid physical standards for special operations units will have precluded such problems but they still must be considered. A great deal of consideration must be given to clothing choice as part of maintaining fighting efficiency. Good headgear, for example, is necessary since up to half of body-heat loss can be through the head. The availability of dry socks is important, too, to prevent trench foot which can occur in cold climates when the feet get wet. British troops operating in the Falklands had to be constantly aware of this danger.

Ground mobility is a particular problem in operations in the Arctic or sub-Arctic, one which is most easily solved by using helicopter insertion as close to the objective as feasible. Care of equipment is very important as well since a mistake which renders an important piece of equipment inoperable in extreme cold weather may well result in the death of an entire patrol.

To achieve mobility in snow and ice, helicopters, wheeled vehicles, tracked vehicles, snowmobiles, water craft, skis, and snowshoes may all have to be used. Finding an enemy will normally be followed up by air strikes since mounting a rapid reaction ground force may be difficult. As in the desert, night operations will normally be preferable since movement may be easily detected against the snow. However, movement at night will normally place operators in even more extreme cold. Adjustments will have to be made, too, since in northern areas nights are extremely long in the winter and short in the summer. Also, as in the desert, attacks against an enemy's lines of communication can contribute to his defeat, especially since alternative routes may not be available. Special operations troops in northern areas must be skilled at deception operations since concealment will be more difficult; hence, leading an enemy astray can contribute to mission success. Another consideration when operating in arctic conditions is that personnel are very dependent upon adequate shelter; hence, protecting their shelter is important for the special operators, while attacks which destroy their shelter can contribute to the elements destroying the enemy.

When evaluating the environmental considerations, the long hours of daylight in the summer and the long hours of nights in winter as well as the extreme cold are all critical considerations; however, it must be remembered as well that during spring and autumn, mud will make operations extremely difficult. As a result, the most suitable time for operations is normally from midwinter until early spring. This time period will allow well-trained and well-equipped troops the most mobility. Nevertheless, many problems remain, including the need for special heavy winter clothing and the requirement of fuel for warmth and survival. Concealment is difficult because of tracks left in the snow and 'ice-fog' created by a heat source. The combination of terrain features which blend into a sea of white, few landmarks, and fog and blowing snow make navigation to an objective difficult (though GPS has greatly alleviated this problem). In addition to mud in the spring, operations in low areas will be impeded by swamps and streams. On the positive side, though, special operators may be able to use small boats to move quickly along waterways once the ice has thawed. In the autumn, rains which create mud can complicate movement during the warmth of the day, when vehicles will create deep ruts, which then freeze at night and can break wheels or axles if vehicles are driven over them. In summer, heavy forest and fallen trees can impede movement in areas of northern woodland.

Amphibious operations in northern areas will encounter other problems. Sea ice may prove a danger to small boats; therefore, it is advisable to carry out landings when visibility is relatively good. The advantages of a landing in the dark must be weighed against the dangers from ice. Any operations from the sea will increase the danger of hypothermia substantially so waterproof clothing must be worn by any personnel operating from boats. Hypothermia is also a danger when operating on inland waterways in cold weather, especially since the current is normally swift, and rivers and streams often contain sand bars. Because the water is so cold in northern rivers, streams, and lakes, personnel who are trained to operate in these areas must practise drills for quickly getting out of the water and out of wet clothing should they fall in.

Combat swimmer operations in northern waters are even more difficult and require special training and equipment. Normally, all personnel operating in cold weather wear layered clothing, but it is even more important for combat swimmers or naval infantry. US Navy SEALs use a system of seven layers which they add or subtract to fit the mission and the weather. This clothing system allows them to operate in temperatures down to minus fifty degrees Fahrenheit. The SEALs even have a special cold-weather pack which is designed to allow snowshoes to be strapped to one side and swimming fins to the other! For actual surface swimming in northern waters, combat swimmers normally use a dry suit with latex wrist and neck seals and a waterproof zipper. Feet coverings are built into the suit. Other clothing may be worn over this suit when not actually swimming or clothing may be worn under it so that a swimmer will already be in camouflage when the dry suit is removed. Once combat swimmers are out of the water they must work quickly to warm themselves up, five to six minutes being considered about the maximum they can take getting out of wet clothing and into dry warm clothing, drying themselves off, drinking hot liquids, and getting into their sleeping bags under shelter. Normally, swimmers are taught to work in teams to get shelters set up and a brew going.

Air support is very important to special operations in northern areas, yet whiteouts can make such operations almost impossible. In addition to whiteout 'greyout' is a problem: it appears over a snow-covered surface during twilight conditions or when the sun is close to the horizon. This can create conditions which impede depth perception, making it difficult to land a helicopter or even to move effectively on skis or snowshoes.

When selecting helicopter LZs in arctic conditions, frozen lakes make one of the best sites; however, members of the special operations team must carry out a ground reconnaissance to check ice thickness and obstructions. Normally, an ice thickness of ten inches or more is desirable. Care must be taken as well since some northern lakes are subject to overflow from nearby streams which creates a mushy surface. Once a helipad is selected, it should be marked with an object which contrasts with the snow or ice to aid the pilot's depth perception. The helicopter pilot must be aware of special problems when landing on frozen surfaces. For example, when landing on a frozen lake, he should not shut down until he is absolutely sure that the ice will hold the chopper. When planning helicopter insertions, the bulky clothing worn by the flight personnel as well as the special operations team and the extra equipment needed for survival must be taken into consideration. The payload for the helicopter may be reduced as well due to the installation of skis or floats.

Northern climates will affect airborne insertions, as well. As with helicopter transport, the number of personnel who can be inserted from smaller aircraft will be severely limited due to the heavier clothing worn and the additional equipment. US Special Forces doctrine calls for a reduction by one-third of the number of troops who may be parachuted into an arctic area of operations. Care must be taken not to overheat the personnel who will be jumping into frigid temperatures so aircraft cabin temperatures should be kept at forty degrees Fahrenheit or below.

Normally a tent or tents, stoves, fuel, and rations will have to be dropped separately. Special operations personnel trained for arctic operations must practise parachuting into snow as well so they are aware of proper landing techniques.

Since mobility or lack thereof is such a critical issue in operations in the Arctic, it is important to have some concept of how depth of snow affects movement. As a general rule, if the snow is less than a foot deep, men on foot or wheeled vehicles can move with difficulty, though men on snowshoes or tracked vehicles will find it easier. Depths of two to two-and-a-half feet will normally slow even tracked vehicles, though low-ground pressure tracked vehicles can operate fairly well. Once two and one-half feet in depth is exceeded even tracked vehicles will normally be immobilised and only special vehicles such as snowmobiles will operate.

For individual movement over snow, skis or snowshoes are highly desirable. If any distance must be travelled skis offer the greatest advantage. Not only can a trained military skier cover four kph over flat terrain, but he will use far less energy than with snowshoes. Current military skis used by US special operations forces are double cambered (cambers are bows in the ski which flatten out when weight is put on them) and use a standard NATO all-metal binding, which can be fitted to a variety of boots. Military ski poles are designed to that they may be converted to avalanche probes very quickly. Special operations skiers are often issued 'climbing skins' which attach to the bottom of the skis, thus allowing the skier to slide forward but not back. Skins are useful for towing loads or for ascending moderate to steep terrain.

For raids, skis are essential since they allow operators to get in and out more quickly. To aid in rapid engagement of the enemy while on skis special operations units normally quickly learn to use their crossed ski poles as a rifle rest or to drop to one knee for a stable shooting platform. Special operations troops train for skijoring, the technique of being towed behind vehicles on skis which allows rapid cross-country movement using a minimum of vehicles.

When moving on foot through snow a team will normally have one or two men moving ahead to act as trailbreakers, but team members should rotate this assignment frequently so no one gets too fatigued. Sleds for carrying equipment should be an integral part of the Table of Organisation & Equipment (TO & E) of any special operations unit operating in the far north.

For operations on ice caps or glaciers, it is necessary to have ex-perienced mountaineers among the special operations troops who can mark trails or act as leaders when it is necessary to climb. Within the SAS, the Mountain Troops would perform this function as would the Royal Marines Arctic and Mountain Warfare Cadre or US Special Forces detachments which specialise in mountain warfare.

Glaciers may not be the only ice to be traversed as frozen waterways often allow easier movement than deep snow. Movement over ice, whether glacier or frozen waterway, will normally require personnel trained to evaluate ice characteristics and its safety. Normally, to support troops moving individually over frozen lakes or streams, about one-and-a-half to two inches of ice is necessary. If required to cross frozen waterways without a chance for a recce, the standard technique is to rope the leading trailbreaker to other personnel and have him crawl ahead and drive an ice axe into the ice at arm's length. If the ice seems solid, he advances about five yards and drives the ice in again.

When choosing routes, ease of movement must be balanced against the availability of natural cover to shield against aerial reconnaissance. Steep slopes should be avoided as should precipitous ravines, unfrozen swamps, open streams, and other obstacles. When choosing routes in the winter, it is better to choose lower terrain, while in the summer it is advisable to follow ridge lines which will normally offer more solid ground. When planning routes and estimating travel time, in low temperatures it must be factored in that shelters and stoves for heating them must be transported and will require time for setting up and taking down. Although transporting the tent and heating devices does require time and effort, it is actually quicker and easier than constructing improvised shelters from local materials.

When planning special operations in the Arctic or sub-Arctic, the primary considerations can be summarised in the following list:

- *Low population density* Since settlements or supply depots will be limited and widely dispersed, access to them can be essential for any major troop concentrations. As a result, raids against such facilities can severely limit an enemy's capability to wage war in the area.
- *Roads and railway lines* Normally year-round roads and railway lines will be very limited and, hence, present a very appealing target for raids by special operations forces.
- *Lakes and waterways* Operationally, lakes and waterways can offer advantages and disadvantages. During the colder months when ice is sufficiently thick, they can be easily crossed or even used to land helicopters or light aircraft. During summer, however, glacier-fed lakes and waterways may receive a great

Use of skis allows special operators to move much more quickly in northern regions (USAF).

volume of water and will have to be traversed using boats.

- *Mapping* Maps of northern areas are often unreliable or lack detail necessary for operational use. Aerial maps combined with GPS can aid special operators to navigate to their objectives more effectively.
- *Navigation* Lack of landmarks, large forested areas, reduced visibility at various times, difficulty of cross-country movement, and magnetic declinations which affect compass readings contribute to difficulties in navigating to objectives. Once again, GPS can be invaluable.
- *Weather* Weather must be considered in the overall context of the mission but can also affect tactics. For example, an attacker or a defender who has the wind at his back during a snowstorm has the advantage.
- *Forests* Areas with heavy forest coverage conceal the special operations unit and allow it to carry out raids, then retreat back into the forest. Forests can also act as a windbreak and offer some protection during snow storms. On the negative side, movement will be slowed through a forest and during the summer forest fires may present a danger.
- *Snow cover* For well-trained troops equipped with snowmobiles, skis, and snowshoes, snow cover can actually help movement, but without proper equipment they will get bogged down and will lose most of their mobility.
- *Ice cover* As has previously been discussed, the freezing of rivers, lakes, and swamps will normally speed movement.
- *Extreme cold* Any unit operating in extreme cold must have proper clothing, shelter and heating, and sufficient food to produce the calories the body needs to warm itself. Windchill will greatly affect how long troops can operate in the open and how far they can move without getting into shelter and warming up. Training for operations in extreme cold is very important as well.
- *Sudden weather changes* Teams must be prepared for sudden changes in temperature as well as snow storms, strong winds, and dense fog. Having access to reliable meteorological information can sometimes allow a special operations unit to take advantage of the local weather or at least avoid being surprised by it.
- *Daylight and darkness* Teams must use the long nights during the winter to cover operations and must factor in the long days

during summer.

- *Seasonal climate changes* Spring thaws and autumn freezes must be factored into any planning for operations during these periods.
- *Atmospheric disturbances* These can affect communications.
- *Effects on individual personnel* The extreme weather conditions will affect response times and stamina of all personnel and any operations must take these factors into consideration.
- *Air support* Any fire support is likely to come from tactical air strikes and resupply will most likely come via air as well. Therefore, special operations planning must consider the availability of air support and must allow for the possibility that weather will hinder such support.

It has already been mentioned that deception may be one of the best defences for special operations units carrying out long-range reconnaissance in arctic/northern environments. Among the techniques which may prove useful are:

- leaving false ski or snowshoe trails to mislead an enemy as to the size of the unit and its direction of movement
- reinforcing track discipline, such as moving in single-file to make the number of troops hard to determine and to limit the number of trails; this technique also makes movement somewhat easier on those following the leaders since they will not have to break the trail
- starting only those fires required for survival; fires started in dry tree stumps will make them less obvious since snow will not melt in as wide an area and also make them easier to start
- booby-trapping trails or leaving behind snipers to slow anyone following the special operations team (the Finns made excellent use of this technique against the Russians during the Winter War)
- siting camps for the special operations team in heavily wooded areas if possible
- using darkness, fog, or falling snow to conceal movement whenever possible, and avoiding open areas, e.g., forest clearings
- being aware of light in the long periods of darkness in the winter and of the tendency of sound to travel a long way in cold, crisp air

A couple of other useful notes for special operations units operating in the far north relate to offensive and defensive operations. If the unit has a mission which includes carrying out raids against the enemy, then the weather should be used to help grant surprise. Attacking out of falling snow, blizzards, or fog gives the special operations unit an even greater advantage of surprise and makes pursuit much more difficult; however, the unit will have to be very well trained in winter warfare to take advantage of these conditions.

The stretched lines of communication in the Arctic create opportunities for sabotage which can greatly hinder enemy operations. For example, blasting gaping holes in the ice of waterways can create barriers or eliminate a route used by the enemy for motorised transport. Destroying bridges may bring enemy supply to a halt since engineer troops will have far more difficulty in rebuilding a bridge in northern climates. Roadblocks may also be created by using explosives to create rock and snow slides or by using timber. Boobytraps and mines near the roadblock can slow repair crews as can ambushes and snipers.

When establishing a defensive position, normally the high ground is even more desirable than usual in arctic terrain since attacking uphill in the snow is especially difficult. Snow and ice can be used to make effective breastworks when creating a defensive position. Six-and-a-half feet of packed snow will normally stop rifle or machine-gun fire as will three-and-a-half feet of ice. Snow also has a dampening effect on artillery or mortar fire rendering impact bursts much less effective.

Whether on the attack or in defence, special operations personnel must take particular care with their weapons in arctic climates. At the most basic level care must be taken not to touch bare skin to the metal parts of the rifle or machine-gun. Additionally, care must be taken when in the firing position not to touch the side of the uncovered face on the weapon. Special care must be taken, too, in maintaining and lubricating the weapon so that the oil does not freeze, rendering the weapon inoperable. Muzzle covers to keep snow and ice from the bore of weapons should be used. Operators must be aware, as well, that bringing their weapons into a warm shelter can result in condensation or the melting of snow on the weapon, thus making the weapon likely to freeze up when back in the cold. Keeping the weapons just outside the tent or shelter but near at hand is one method for preventing this problem as is cleaning them when they are taken into a shelter.

Although the same special operations troops who are trained for arctic/cold-weather warfare also receive mountain training, many additional skills are required. Among the skills necessary for special operations in the mountains are rock and ice climbing, rappelling, belaying, and negotiating different types of obstacles. However, not all operators will have equal skill levels so the best mountaineers will normally receive extra training to act as mountain leaders or mountain guides who will scale the hardest cliff faces or ice faces and establish belays and ropes to assist other team members.

Personnel also learn techniques for walking in mountains, techniques which make movement easier, quieter, and safer. Balance is very important so the operator's weight is centred over the feet at all times. The foot should be placed flat on the ground to obtain as much contact with the ground as possible. Moderate steps at a steady pace are better than longer steps. However, the more adverse the conditions, the slower the pace should be. Normally, a moderate pace should allow breaks to be kept to a minimum, but when they are taken it is better to rest on level ground. About half an hour after mountain movement begins, a break to adjust packs and boot laces is a good idea.

For steeper slopes, military mountaineers learn what is usually called the 'rest step.' Used primarily for steep slopes, snowfields, and at higher elevations, the rest step controls the pace and limits fatigue by allowing a short time for recuperation between steps. After each slow rhythmic step forward, the operator should pause briefly and relax the muscles of the forward leg while resting his weight on the rear leg which is kept straight with the knee locked so bone is supporting the weight. He should synchronise his breathing with each step, with more difficult terrain requiring more deep breaths per step.

Downhill walking requires less energy than uphill walking but is harder on the body since each step down on an incline puts the body weight on the feet and legs. Tighter boot laces can help the boot to brace the leg, and use of a ski pole, ice axe, or walking stick can take some of the load and add stability. Whenever possible, travelling on the sides of hills should be avoided as there is too much chance of twisted ankles, back injuries, or falls. When the sides of hills must be traversed, lower-angle flat areas such as rocks, animal trails, or the ground above brush clumps should be used.

When moving across snow slopes, various specialised walking techniques may be employed as well. The diagonal traverse technique is very efficient for ascending in snow. Basically a two-step sequence, the diagonal traverse uses a basic rest step with the leading foot placed uphill and the weight on the downhill foot. The ice axe is then placed in the snow ahead of the lead foot and used as a lever as weight is shifted to the lead foot and the rear foot is brought ahead and the process is repeated. Step kicking is another technique which is useful for moving through soft snow on moderate slopes. In this technique, the operator swings his foot into the snow so the weight and momentum of the boot create a step in the snow. These steps should be angled in towards the slope slightly to be more secure. Operators following the trailbreaker will use the 'steps' he has created. For descending a snow slope that is too steep for normal steps, then the 'plunge step' is used. In the plunge step, the operator steps off and plants his foot solidly by driving his heel into the snow while keeping the leg straight. Once this foot is planted he shifts his weight to it and steps off with the other foot. On very steep terrain it may be necessary to squat on the leg taking the weight when getting ready for the plunge step. When using this technique the upper body should be kept erect or leaning slightly forward.

When travelling across snow it is normally advisable to use a different descent route from the ascent route. It is useful, too, to watch for dirty snow as it absorbs heat better and thus hardens faster than clean snow. In the northern hemisphere, slopes with southern or western exposure will offer firmer walking surfaces earlier in the season but will also be more prone to avalanches in the spring. If daytime temperatures are above freezing, it is better to travel late at night or early in the morning so the snow's surface will be harder. Operators should avoid walking next to logs, trees, and rocks where the subsurface snow may have melted creating hidden pitfalls.

Other conditions encountered on slopes require adjustment in walking technique as well. For example, when moving through thick brush it is best to take the most direct route across, look for fallen trees which may be used as raised paths through the brush, or to create a tunnel through it by prising the brush apart. Brush does offer concealment from observation. A scree slope comprised of small rocks can be quite slippery and difficult, but by using a step similar to the 'kick step' for snow when ascending (and taking care not to slip) an operator can make it up scree. For descending scree, short, shuffling steps are best. An ice axe can be used to aid both ascent and descent in scree. Talus slopes which are comprised of larger rocks should be traversed on the uphill side of rocks and operators must stay alert for movement under foot.

However, sometimes knowing how to walk on a mountain is not enough, and climbing techniques must be employed. When possible, steep rock faces will usually be avoided, but sometimes a steep face offers an unexpected route to a target and, therefore, might be unguarded or lightly guarded. If it is necessary to scale a steep face, the lead climber will first do the climb in his mind after studying possible routes to the top looking for cracks, ledges, nubbins, and other irregularities in the rock that offer handholds and footholds. He will also look for larger ledges or other points where the team may rest during the ascent. Only after going over the route step-by-step mentally will the lead climber be ready to begin his ascent.

When actually climbing rock faces, the operator must use hands, feet, and body in coordination. The body is nearly vertical with weight centred over both feet in the correct climbing stance. The normal climbing sequence will proceed in steps beginning with a shift in weight from both feet to one foot so the other foot can be lifted. Once the unweighted foot is lifted and placed in a new position no more than two feet from the starting position so the operator is not thrown off balance, then the weight is shifted once again to both feet. The sequence is then repeated with the foot which initially remained planted. Next, the body is lifted into a new two-legged stance, and the hands are moved to a new hold to balance and stabilise the body. Holds should be checked to make sure the rock is solid before depending on them. Note, by the way, that the term 'holds' can refer to rests for the feet as well as hands. The basic precept, however, is to climb with the feet and use the hands for balance. It is important, too, that the feet maintain maximum sole contact with the rock.

Skilful climbers combine techniques for more difficult situations. Mantling, for example, is used when the distance between holds is so great that there are no places to move the hands or feet nearby. If there is a ledge above the operator's head, though, he can hook both hands over the ledge and hoist himself until his head is above his hands at which point he is pushing himself up, rotating his hands inward at the same time to place his palms more securely on the ledge. Once his arms are locked and he has lifted himself as high as possible, he can raise a foot and place it on the ledge, then use an arm to reach a hold not previously available. It is also possible to walk the feet up the rock face to take some weight off the arms during mantling, but obviously upper body strength is very important.

'Stemming' is another technique which can be very useful for the military mountaineer. In this technique, the feet are in a relatively wide stance and work in opposition as they press against resistance on each side. Stemming is used most often in chimneys (parallel cracks at least one foot apart, just big enough to allow the body to squeeze through). By pushing outwards with hands and feet against the sides of the crack, friction is created. By alternately moving the hands and feet up the crack the operator can ascend. In wider chimneys, the back and buttocks may be used to apply pressure opposite the feet and the ascent may be made by walking the feet up and sliding the back up alternately.

When descending on steep rock faces, ropes are normally used, but if necessary skilled climbers can descend without ropes. Normally, on easier terrain, the operator will face out so that he can see the route better, but as the descent becomes more difficult he may have to turn sideways, which will still let him see the route while still using hands and feet on any holds. On steep descents, the operator will have to face the rock and apply his climbing skill. Holds are less visible when climbing down and slips are more likely; hence, the climber will have to lean well away from the rock to look for holds and plan his next movements. More weight is usually placed on handholds during a descent as the operator lowers himself to his next foothold. Hands should be moved to holds as low as the waist if possible to allow more range of movement in reaching the next foothold. But the climber must not overextend himself, as this will force him to release his handholds before reaching the next foothold.

For more difficult climbs, it may be necessary to use a rope. The selection of ropes for mountain operations is very important, with two types commonly used by US troops: nylon-laid ropes (stranded ropes) and kernmantle ropes (plaited around a core). The nylon-laid ropes can be used for most tasks and are cheaper but less durable than kernmantle ropes. Many mountain-trained units will have two types of kernmantle rope available, dynamic and static. The dynamic version will stretch between eight and twelve per cent of its length and will normally be used for ascending or descending. The static version only has about two per cent of stretch and will be used for rope bridges or fixed ropes.

Mountain troops normally learn basic rules of rope care, including:

- thorough inspection of ropes prior to use as well as during and after use to find cuts, frays, abrasions, mildew, soft spots, or worm spots
- hanging wet ropes to drip dry on a rounded wooden peg at room temperature: heat should not be applied
- avoiding stepping on the rope or dragging it on the ground unnecessarily
- taking care not to run the rope over sharp or rough edges: it may be necessary to pad it
- keeping ropes away from oil, acids, or other corrosives
- avoid running ropes across one another when under tension to avoid damaging them
- not leaving rope knotted or under tension any longer than necessary
- cleaning ropes in cool water, loosely coiling them, and hanging them to dry out of direct sunlight as ultraviolet rays can harm synthetic fibres
- storing ropes in a cool, dry, shaded area on a peg

Learning knot-tying is another important aspect of military mountaineering. As a side note, when undergoing climbing training, a friend of the author's who was a US Navy SEAL had to adjust to tying knots out of the water since SEALs learn their basic knot tying while submerged without oxygen. This technique builds speed and lung power, but the SEAL found it odd tying knots on dry land while he could breathe!

The knots normally taught as part of basic mountaineering training and their uses are:

- *square knot* used for tying two ropes of equal diameter; note, this knot is always secured with an overhand knot
- *round-turn two half-hitches* used to tie the end of a rope to an anchor
- *end-of-the-rope clove-hitch* used as an intermediate anchor knot which requires constant tension
- *middle-of-the-rope clove-hitch* used to secure the middle of a rope to an anchor
- *rappel-seat (left- or right-hand brake)* used in conjunction with a karabiner to form a rope harness for rappelling (abseiling)
- *figure-of-eight loop* used to form a fixed loop in the end of a rope or anywhere along the length of the rope; fixed loops are left large enough to insert a karabiner
- *rerouted figure-of-eight knot* used to attach a climber to the climbing rope with two ropes running parallel
- *figure-of-eight slip knot* used to form an adjustable loop in the middle of a rope
- *end-of-the-rope prusik* used to attach a movable rope to a fixed one
- *middle-of-the-rope prusik* used to attach a movable rope to a fixed rope anywhere along the length of the fixed rope
- *bowline on a coil* used to secure a climber to the end of a climbing rope

Of course, knowing how to tie the knots must be combined with an understanding of when each should be used and how to properly employ them during a climb or descent. Special operations troops who may not be able to travel with full climbing gear, for example, may use the knot skills to 'tie-in' to the climbing rope, though this technique offers little support to the climber. Prefabricated harnesses give the operator more support and are safer, but are more bulky and may not fit in the pack. The three primary types of prefabricated harness are: seat harness, chest harness, and full-body harness. A compromise between tying in to the rope and a pre-made harness is the improvised harness which can be constructed of rope and webbed gear. An improvised seat harness, for example, can be constructed from a twenty-five foot length of webbing. At least some special operations units trained for mountain operations have webbed gear which is designed to double as rappel or climbing harness.

Another important skill for military mountaineering is the use of the belay. Belaying is a method for applying friction to a rope, thus controlling the amount of rope that is paid out or taken in. In the military application, especially, it is used to arrest a climber who has fallen or to control the rate of descent of a load when lowering it. Belaying will ensure that if one man falls during a rope ascent or descent he does not take the rest of the team with him. The belay man must be anchored into the rock face to prevent him from being pulled out of his position if pull is suddenly exerted. Belays may be of the body type in which a rope is passed around the belayer's body, thus creating friction. The body belay may be rigged with the belayer standing or sitting, with the latter usually considered the most stable. Mechanical belays may also be rigged employing devices designed for use in constructing a belay. The belayer must be able to perform three basic tasks: first, manipulate the rope so that the climber has enough slack during movement, second, take up the rope when necessary to remove extra slack, and third, apply the brake to halt a fall. He must retain total control of the rope at all times and *never* remove the brake hand from the rope. The belay man normally is trained to respond to the basic mountaineering commands, which are:

- *Break!* tells the belay man to secure the rope and not pay out any more.
- *Slack!* tells the belay man to move so he slackens the rope allowing more to be paid out, but the belay man should not attempt to feed the rope to the climber who must pull the rope he needs.
- *Up rope!* informs the belay man to take up all rope slack between him and the climber or the load, at which point the belay man will move into the brake position.
- *Tension!* tells the belay man to take up all slack between him and the climber or load, pull the rope tight, then go to the brake position.
- *Falling!* This command lets the belay man know that the climber has slipped and that he should apply the brake to arrest his fall.

Lead climbers may be asked to establish rope bridges or suspension traverses to help other members of their team cross glaciers or chasms. When doing so they will normally use tightening systems employing knots such as the figure-of-eight slip and prusiks. Normally static rope rather than dynamic rope will be used.

Although all members of a special operations units trained for mountain operations will learn rock climbing, only the most skilled lead climbers will normally employ balance or free climbing in which hand and foot holds naturally available on the rock face are employed. Lead climbers will usually emplace artificial hand and foot holds to aid follow-on climbers from their team.

Lead climbers, or what the US Army Rangers term 'Assault Climbers', will move ahead of the rest of their team to install fixed ropes, vertical hauling lines, and suspension traverses for other troops to aid them in overcoming mountain obstacles. It is best if there are two lead climbers as they will be able to work more efficiently and quickly. When installing some of these climbing aids it will be necessary to create an A-frame to gain artificial height. For example, vertical hauling lines and suspension traverses will likely require an A-frame.

The vertical hauling line, which is used to move men or equipment up a vertical or near vertical slope may be used in conjunction with a fixed rope. When establishing a vertical hauling line, the assault climbers must consider:

- the most suitable location
- the availability of anchors (both natural and artificial)
- the presence of good loading and off-loading platforms
- sufficient clearance for the load
- whether an A-frame is needed to gain artificial height
- using a hauling-line to haul personnel and equipment up and down the slope
- using a pulley or locking karabiner on the A-frame to ease friction on the hauling line
- using a knotted hand-line to assist personnel in movement up the slope
- placement of personnel at top and bottom to monitor safe procedures

Because they are so widely used in military mountaineering, it is important to have a sound knowledge of anchors since failure of any rope system is most likely to occur at the anchor point. Normally, these failures occur because of poor terrain features which are not really suitable for an anchor point or placing equipment used in rigging the anchor improperly or in insufficient numbers.

When selecting natural anchors, which have the advantage of already being in place, care must be taken to establish their strength and stability before using them. The climbing rope may be tied directly to the anchor, but normally a sling is attached to the anchor, then the climbing rope is attached to the sling with a karabiner. The following are important considerations when selecting natural anchors:

- *Trees* In forested terrain, trees are widely used, but they must be checked carefully for suitability. Since trees normally have shallow root-systems in rocky terrain, the operator should push and pull on the tree vigorously to make sure it will stay put. Anchoring as low on the tree as possible will prevent too much leverage being applied to the tree. When trees are producing sap, padding can be used to keep it off of the slings and ropes.
- *Boulders* Rocks which are sunk deeply in the ground can make excellent anchors, but they must be tapped with a piton hammer to check solidness. Loose rock formations are not stable. Scree fields are also indicators that rocks in that area are probably not solid. When placing the rope or sling, any areas of the rock which are sharp and might abrade it should be padded.
- *Chockstones* These are rocks that are wedged into a crack which narrows downward. Chockstones must be checked for strength and security, especially crumbling. They should be well tested before use to be sure they are solid enough and strong enough

Figure 8   Use of a chockstone as an anchor. Note that the chockstones are often directional: i.e., a pull in one direction will be secure while a pull in the other will not. In this illustration, the chockstone should be secure against a downward pull but might come loose if pulled outward. Note that the sling is well-centred on the chockstone to distribute weight evenly and to make sure it does not become abraided by being caught between the chockstone and the chock.

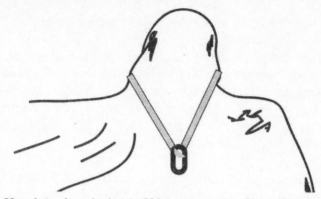

Figure 9   Use of a rock projection (nubbin) as an anchor. If a nubbin is used, its firmness must be tested to make sure it will stay in place. The rock should also be checked for cracks or other signs of weakness. If there are sharp edges then the sling should be padded.

to support the load. It is important to check that they have sufficient surface contact and are tapered so that they will remain in position. Three important points to bear in mind are that chockstones may be solid if pulled in one direction but will pull free if pulled in another; that the operator can make his own chockstones by wedging a rock into position, tying on a rope, and attaching a karabiner; and that slings should not be wedged between the chockstone and the rock wall to prevent a fall from cutting the webbing runner.

- *Rock projections* Often called 'nubbins', these are rocks which project enough to allow attachment of a harness. They can be used as anchor points, but must be checked for cracks, weathering, or other weakness.
- *Tunnels and arches* These holes formed in solid rock are one of the most secure anchor points since the rope/sling may be pulled in any direction. Before threading a sling through a load-bearing hole, it should be checked for sharp edges, which should be padded if encountered.
- *Bushes and shrubs* Though the least desirable natural anchor, if there is no other choice a rope may be placed around the bases of several bushes. Bushes should be given a tug check to make sure they are well-rooted and the rope should be placed as low as possible.

When using a natural anchor with a sling, three basic methods are used to attach the sling. The 'drape' technique involves hanging or draping the sling over the anchor. The 'wrap' technique involves wrapping the sling around the anchor, then connecting the two ends with a karabiner. The 'girth' technique involves tying the sling around the anchor with a girth hitch, though this method does reduce the strength of the sling somewhat. No matter which of these methods is used the knot should be off to the side so it does not interfere with normal karabiner movement.

It is not always necessary to use a sling. A rope anchor may be used, though it will sacrifice the rope length which is used to tie the anchor. The knot should be placed away form the anchor so that the knot is under less stress. When the rope will be required to bear heavy loads, it can be wrapped around the anchor – normally a minimum of four turns – to absorb tension.

Artificial anchors are used when natural anchors are not available. For special operators, however, natural anchors are often desirable since they will be less noisy and they will leave less trace of passage. Among the most common artificial anchors are:

- *Deadman* This is any anchor created by burying a solid object in the ground. Timbers such as railway sleepers or large boulders can be used but so can skis, ice axes, snowshoes, or other pieces of equipment. In hard, rocky terrain where it is hard to dig a trench to bury the anchor, a deadman anchor can be constructed by placing an anchor as deeply as possible, then stacking rocks around it for strength, though this type of deadman will not normally be as strong as one which is buried.
- *Pitons* Pitons can be driven into rock faces, but skill is necessary to anchor them properly. Among the advantages of pitons are that they can support pulls in multiple directions, are relatively simple, and can be used in very thin cracks where other types of artificial anchors might not work. Disadvantages include the noise created while hammering them in, the possibility of breaking the rock while driving them in, their difficulty of removal, their tendency to leave scars on the rock, and the fact they may be dropped if not tied off during use. Note that many of these disadvantages either can create noise or leave visible traces thus possibly compromising a special operations unit's mission. Piton placement is very critical. As a rule, a piton properly sized for a rock crack will fit a half to two-thirds of the way into the crack before being driven in with the hammer. Prior to inserting a piton the rock should be tested with the hammer to be sure the rock is not soft or rotten. If

there is no choice other than driving the piton into soft rock, then loose debris should be cleared away before driving the piton in completely. While driving the piton it is advisable to attach it to a sling with a karabiner so it will not be lost if knocked out of the crack. The operator placing the piton should make sure that the piton does not spread the rock thus making it insecure. Experience helps an operator choose sound cracks for piton placement. It is a good idea to practise placing pitons with either hand since operationally versatility may be required. Once emplaced, pitons should be tested by inserting a rope into a karabiner attached to the piton, then after grasping the rope half a metre or more from the karabiner, jerk the rope in various directions to make sure it will not move. If there is any doubt of its security, it will be necessary to try elsewhere.

- *Chocks* Instead of using natural chocks, a climber can adjust or insert rocks to wedge them securely, but this technique requires substantial experience to be used safely. The advantages include quiet installation and recovery, ease of retrieval for reuse, ease of carrying, virtually no rock scarring as with pitons, and chocks may be usable where pitons cannot be used. The disadvantages of chocks include the possibility that they will not fit in thin cracks which will accept pitons, are often only secure for pulls in one direction, and that the technique requires a lot of practice and experience. When placing chocks, the technique is to find a crack which is constricted at some point, then place the chock above and behind the constriction. Jerking down on the loop affixed to the chock should set it. When setting the chock as much surface contact as possible is desirable. Chocks should be checked by pulling against them in anticipated directions of pull. To allow chocks to be secure in more directions, pairs of chocks in opposition may be used, but once again this requires experience to properly set them.
- *Spring-loaded camming device* This device is very quick to place and may be easily retrieved. One advantage is that the SLCD may be emplaced using one hand. Another advantage of the SLCD is that it will hold well in parallel-sided cracks. Some care must be exercised in placing the SLCD, however, to be sure that it is aligned in the direction of force to be applied against it. The SLCD must be placed so that the direction of pull is parallel to the shaft.
- *Bolts* Bolts are especially useful where no cracks are available.

Bolts are very secure, but strong rock which is not flaking, crumbling, or cracking is necessary. One disadvantage of the bolt is it requires either a hammer or a drill to be emplaced, both of which will create substantial noise. There are some bolts designed to be 'self-drilling' since they turn as they are hammered, but these still create noise.

Equalising anchors may be used to spread an intended load over multiple anchors. This method of using multiple anchor points provides greater strength for heavier loads but also grants redundancy in case one anchor point fails. A self-equalising anchor is sometimes used when rappelling requiring a chance of lateral direction during the rappel, but this technique should be avoided unless absolutely necessary since if one of the anchor points fails, the shock can cause other anchors to fail. The pre-equalised anchor distributes a load equally at each individual point and is aimed in the direction of the load. By tying an overhand or figure-of-eight knot in the webbing or sling, the anchor is pre-equalised and, thus, prevents extension and shock-loading if one point fails. This prevents other points from failing.

The suspension traverse is normally installed to aid in moving operators and equipment over rivers, ravines, chasms, and up and down a vertical rock face. The considerations for this are much the same as for vertical hauling lines as discussed above.

When lead climbers establish a fixed rope it is intended to assist operators in movement over difficult terrain and to allow them to negotiate dangerous mountain routes more safely and quickly when carrying heavy equipment. It is generally a good idea for an operator to attach himself to the fixed rope with a sling using a friction knot which will slide along the rope as he ascends but which will arrest his fall if he slips. The considerations for establishing a fixed rope include:

- choosing the most suitable location, one which allows ease of negotiation and avoids as many obstacles as possible
- checking the availability of anchors (natural or artificial)
- finding an area safe from falling rock and ice
- identifying the best choice tactically
- routing the rope between the knees and chest high
- ensuring that the rope is fairly tight (except at obstacles which the climber must avoid, in which case the rope should be loose enough to allow movement around the obstacle while remaining safe)

- avoiding the need for the climber to cross over the top of the rope
- selecting an adequate number of intermediate anchor points

Special operations personnel should be well trained in rappelling as they will use this technique not just in mountaineering but in helicopter insertions and during building entries. For purposes of mountaineering, personnel should normally be familiar with:

- *The hasty rappel* This rappel is normally chosen when speed is important and when the descent will be down a moderate pitch. The rope is run across the back with the hand nearest the anchor acting as the guide hand and the other as the brake hand.
- *The body rappel* This rappel is used on steeper pitches and requires the rappeller to face the anchor point and straddle the rope which he then pulls from behind, runs around either hip, then diagonally across the chest, and back over the opposite shoulder. The rope is then run to the brake hand which is on the same side as the hip that the rope crosses. The rapeller leads with the brake hand down and faces slightly sideways. Note that neither of these rappels is used when there is an overhang as both require surface contact of the feet. They do not require a belay from below.
- *The seat-hip rappel* This rappel employs a karabiner inserted in a rope sling seat to absorb friction. Care must be taken when hooking the rope into the karabiner to make sure that it is in correctly and secure to avoid the gate being pushed open by the rope. Care must also be taken that loose clothing or equipment ties are not pulled into the locking karabiner, thus stopping the rappel. A figure-of-eight descender may be used for this rappel as well. This allows a faster descent from an overhang. If there is not a belayer below during the descent, a self-belay may be rigged by knotting the rope. That way if the rapeller needs both hands, he will not lose control of the rope.

The Australian rappel which allows personnel to descend facing downward is also useful for operations where an enemy may be at the base of a rock face.

The first rappeller down will normally be an experienced mountaineer and will have the following responsibilities:

- to choose a smooth route for the rope clear of sharp rocks
- to conduct a self-belay
- to clear the route by moving loose stones out of the way so the rope does not dislodge them
- to ensure the rope reaches the bottom or reaches a point from which additional rappels can be made
- to ensure that the rope will run freely around the rappel point when pulled from below
- to clear the rappel line by straightening twists and tangles
- to belay subsequent rappellers down the rope or monitor other belayers
- to take charge of personnel as they arrive at the bottom and assign them tasks such as perimeter security

When preparing to rappel down a rock face or cliff, the following considerations are important:

- selection of a suitable primary and secondary anchor, then their testing
- that any rappel point has primary and secondary anchors
- that the rappel point has equal tension among all anchor points
- that a double rope is used whenever possible
- that ropes reach the off-load point (platform)
- that the site chosen has suitable on- and off-loading platforms
- that any personnel working near the edge are secured with a safety rope
- that the route chosen is free of loose rock and debris

When actually carrying out the rappel, it is advisable if possible to ensure that the following conditions are met:

- personnel at the top of the rappel point should maintain communications with those at the bottom of the rappel point
- belay men should be used at the bottom of each rope
- operators rappelling should move down the cliff in a controlled descent; although many films of rappelling show personnel 'bounding' down a cliff, this actually stresses the anchor and causes undue wear and friction on the rope
- the rappeller should wear gloves and a helmet
- the rappeller should clear the ropes once his descent is completed

- rappellers might have to 'tie off' during a rappel to stop during the descent; this is accomplished by passing the rope around the body and wrapping it three or more times around the guide-hand-side leg; it may also be tied off using the appropriate knot for the rappel device being used

Note the mention of a helmet. Many special operations troops do not normally use a standard military helmet; however, because of the danger of falling rock during mountain operations, a helmet is highly recommended.

Operationally, special operations teams will most likely have to retrieve their ropes, both for re-use and so as not to show their route to the enemy. There are two basic methods for setting up a retrievable rappel. In the first, the rope is doubled when the rappel is less than half the length of the rope. The loop of the rope is thrown over the anchor point and a clove hitch is tied around a karabiner just below the anchor point. If properly attached, a pull on the portion of the rope to which the karabiner is attached will allow it to slide around the anchor point. When the length of rappel is greater than half the length of the rope, then two ropes can be joined around the anchor point, then hitched as with a single rope.

Although some of the same climbing techniques will apply for traversing snow or ice, on steeper slopes special techniques will be required. An ice axe is a necessity for ascents on snow and ice and crampons (climbing spikes strapped to the boots) are desirable. On steep slopes in deep snow, the operator should climb straight up facing the slope using the ice axe shaft as a self-belay by driving it into the snow as he progresses. It is normally better to climb snow-covered slopes using a traversing movement to conserve energy, though this method should be avoided if there is significant danger of avalanches. Kick steps may be used to gain traction, but when it is difficult to make a step with the boot, the ice axe may be used to create a step. Crampons will make movement faster and easier. When descending on snow, movement should be slow and deliberate. The heels should be kicked into the snow. An ice axe may be jammed into the snow at each step to help keep the body erect and provide additional safety. Crampons or step-cutting will make many descents easier. 'Glissading' may also be used in descents in snow. In simple terms glissading is the use of an intentional slide on the feet or buttocks using the ice axe to guide and brake the glissade. The two basic types of glissade are the 'squatting glissade' and the 'sitting glissade', which are self-explanatory.

During ice movement, the ice axe and crampons are not just desirable but a necessity. The ice axe is very versatile and may be used in the cane position as a third point of contact or a brake, in the cross-body position for balance or self-arrest, in the anchor position with the pick driven into the ice while climbing a steep incline, in the push-hold position with the pick driven into the ice and the top used as a handhold by the climber, the dagger position in which the axe is stabbed into the ice above the shoulder to give a handhold, or in the hammer position to set the pick very deeply on nearly vertical slopes. When climbing nearly vertical slopes, two ice axes may be necessary. Crampons are used in a stride much like that in mountain-walking except that the leg being advanced is swung in a slight arc around the fixed foot to avoid locking the crampons or catching them in clothing. When descending with crampons and ice axe, it is important to be sure the points of the crampons are inserted in the snow or ice and that short steps are taken to minimise the chances of tripping.

The ice axe is very useful for cutting steps and handholds in ice and snow. Lead climbers can cut steps to assist less skilled climbers who will follow them. The ice axe is also invaluable for self-arrest on steep ice. By self-belaying with the ice pick driven well into the ice, a fall is unlikely, but if one does occur a climber must first gain control of his body which may be rolling or spinning. He should get into a position where his head is facing down with his feet pointing down the slope. If crampons are worn, the feet should be raised to they do not dig into the ice and cause the climber to tumble. Once the body is controlled and in the proper position, the ice axe's pick should be driven into the ice, increasing the pressure until the fall is arrested.

The same types of anchors which have previously been discussed for use in climbing may also be used on snow and ice, but with the addition of the 'horseshoe' or 'bollard' anchor. By cutting with the ice axe or stamping with the boots this artificial anchor shaped like a horseshoe may be created in ice or snow. In snow it should be at least ten feet in width and in ice two feet in width. The bollard should be at least twice as long as the width with a trench as deep as possible around the horseshoe. In ice, six inches is the minimum depth. The back side of the anchor should be undercut so the rope does not slip off. This type of anchor must be inspected frequently to make sure the rope is not cutting through the snow or ice and should be used only when other types of anchors are not possible.

An ice axe may also be used as a snow anchor, or it can be used as a belay in conjunction with the belayer's boot. After driving the handle of the ice axe deeply into the snow, the belayer places his uphill foot against the downhill side of the axe for support. The rope is then looped around the ice over the boot. To brake, the belayer can wrap the rope around the heel of the boot.

Movement over glaciers is quite dangerous and should only be attempted if there is no other possible route. Operators crossing glaciers face ice falls, ice avalanches, and crevasses. Snow-covered crevasses make movement extremely hazardous. Roped movement is necessary on glaciers to provide an added margin of safety should one member slip or fall. Since a team member who does fall into a crevasse will probably hang for a time while awaiting rescue by his comrades, some type of seat/chest combination harness is advisable.

When crossing crevasses, narrow cracks can be jumped as long as the take-off and landing points offer solid footing. Sometimes, too, an ice bridge will be strong enough to support an operator, but it must be tested carefully. The real danger in crevasses is that a climber will fall into a snow-covered one that is not visible. Probing ahead of the team with the shaft of an ice axe may be necessary where it is suspected that a 'snow bridge' has been formed over a crevasse. If the haft does not meet resistance, then a crevasse is indicated. Special collapsible probes which are longer than the haft of an ice axe are even better for checking ahead of movement near possible snow-filled crevasses. Any teams operating on glaciers must be well-drilled in techniques of belaying should an operator start to fall into a crevasse since if the fall is stopped quickly he will be able to climb out himself while being belayed.

Mountain special operations units must have at least some training in mountain rescue and evacuation in case they are sent in to rescue downed aircrews, to assist another unit which has suffered casualties, or to evacuate a team member who has been injured. One of the first tasks special operations personnel will have to perform upon arriving at the scene for a rescue is to evaluate the circumstances to determine whether additional personnel and/or equipment is needed; how serious the casualties are and whether specialised medical personnel are needed; what the weather conditions are and how they will affect the rescue effort; whether the terrain is hazardous; and how much time is available (this will vary according to factors such as the weather, enemy activity, or the condition of casualties).

If it is not possible to get helicopters in, then the operators must be able to plan an evacuation route and safely transport a casualty or casualties using their climbing techniques; however, the need to get a casualty to medical care quickly must not compromise safety as everyone could perish or be injured. Blankets and waterproof gear must be available for casualities. Before moving a casualty, broken bones should be immobilised and dressings should be applied and reinforced. Operators should be trained in various transport methods for casualties, including those which require the use of ropes to secure them to an operator's back. The special operations evacuation team may have to use 'buddy rappel' techniques too, with a casualty on their backs in order to get him down a cliff face. Normally, the operators will be trained in making impromptu litters to help transport casualties and to allow them to be lowered down cliffs. Belay techniques can be used when operators are carrying a litter up or down a slope so that much of the weight of the litter is actually being taken by a rope and pulley.

Military mountaineering training prepares operators to function as part of a an arctic and mountain warfare team, but normally within special operations units there will be other operators who have received more advanced training so that they can take the lead in especially difficult situations. As a result, it is useful to look at the qualifications expected of operators at different levels of training. The following skill levels are those specified for three different levels of mountain warfare skill in the US armed forces:

1 *Basic mountaineer* These graduates of a basic mountaineering course have the ability to operate in mountain terrain under the supervision of those with more advanced training. They will not be qualified to act as lead climbers. The basic mountaineer should acquire knowledge of the following:
   - the characteristics of the mountain environment in both summer and winter
   - mountaineering safety
   - the use, care, and packing of individual cold-weather clothing and equipment
   - the care and use of basic mountaineering equipment
   - mountain bivouac techniques
   - mountain communications
   - mountain travel and walking techniques
   - hazard recognition and route selection
   - mountain navigation
   - basic medical evacuation
   - rope management and knots
   - the use of anchors, natural and artificial
   - belay and rappel techniques
   - the use of fixed ropes
   - rock climbing fundamentals
   - rope bridges and lowering systems
   - individual movement on snow and ice

- mountain stream crossings and water survival techniques
- first aid for mountain illnesses and injuries

2 *Assault climber* The assault climber is responsible for rigging and maintaining rope systems and in using specialised mountaineering equipment. He is also capable of rigging complex, multipoint anchors and high angle lifting or lowering systems. Preferably, special operations personnel assigned to specialised mountain units will achieve this level as soon as possible. In addition to those skills learned at level 1, the assault climber will have added the following:
- the use of specialised mountaineering equipment
- multipitch climbing, free climbing, and aid climbing
- multipitch rappelling
- the establishment and operation of hauling systems
- the establishment of fixed ropes with intermediate anchors
- movement on moderate-angle snow and ice
- the establishment of evacuation systems, including high-angle rescues
- avalanche hazard evacuation and rescue techniques
- movement on glaciers

3 *Mountain leader* In addition to all of this training, the mountain leader will have extensive practical experience in a variety of mountain environments in all seasons of the year. Mountain leaders will also normally be in charge of training for members of their units and can act as instructors at mountain training facilities. In addition to level 1 and level 2 skills, the mountain leader will be capable of the following:
- the recognition and evaluation of special terrain, weather, and hazards
- the preparation of route, movement, bivouac, and risk management plans for all conditions and elevation levels
- carrying out roped movement techniques on steep snow and ice
- multipitch climbing on mixed terrain (rock, snow, and ice)
- glacier travel and crevasse rescue
- the establishment and operation of technical high-angle, multipitch rescue and evacuation systems
- the use of winter shelters and survival techniques
- leading units over technically difficult, hazardous, or exposed terrain in both winter and summer conditions

The ability to build a shelter from available materials will often help the special operator survive.

Jungle

Jungles can normally be divided into tropical rain forests in which large trees have branches which form canopies on two or three different levels and deciduous forests which are in semitropical zones and normally do not have the density of trees of the rain forest. Foot movement is normally easier in the rain forest, though visibility is very limited. Aerial observation

Special operators often train and work with indigenous personnel such as these Contra rebels in Central America.

is very difficult in the rain forest and vehicular movement is virtually impossible. Heavier undergrowth in the deciduous forest limits ground foot movement, but observation is easier both on the ground and from the air. Operations may take place in secondary jungles which are on the edges of rain forests or deciduous forests or in areas where most of the jungle has been cleared. Undergrowth is typically very heavy in secondary jungle limiting movement and observation.

Swamps are likely to be encountered in lower jungle areas where there is water and poor drainage. In coastal areas, mangrove swamps restrict movement and observation. Palm swamps, which can exist in fresh or salt water, also restrict movement and observation. Both types of swamp offer excellent concealment from the air. If the special operations unit is acting as a guerrilla force, swamps offer a good haven, but if they are hunting guerrillas, then swamps hinder operations.

In some jungles there will be savannahs, broad, open grassland with few trees, but with thick, broad-bladed grass up to five metres high. Foot movement is slow through savannahs and ground observation is not usually good, but it is easy to detect movement from the air.

Normally, there will be some cultivated areas in jungles, often a way of locating guerrillas from the air but also an indication of where the local population can be found. Rice paddies usually inhibit movement but offer good fields of fire and observation. Larger plantations where tree crops such as rubber or coconuts are grown are normally well tended and allow ease of movement and observation. The number of workers on plantations means special operations units attempting clandestine movement through them must be careful. There may also be small farms which are usually abandoned after a couple of years and become overgrown.

In the jungle, operators must be aware of the special hazards they will face, including heavy rains during the rainy season and high heat and humidity. Mosquitoes which carry malaria are a constant danger and those operating in jungle environments will normally be taking dapsone or other preventative drugs. Other stinging and biting insects can inflict painful and irritating injuries. Leeches are an annoyance as well as a a possible source of infection. Operators will normally use 'leech straps' which are wrapped around the lower legs to prevent leeches reaching the crotch. If an operator does have attached leeches they should not be pulled off. Instead, they should be touched with insect repellent, alcohol, or a burning ember or cigarette. Snake bites are another possible danger in the jungle, especially since some jungle snakes are particularly poisonous. Special operations units in the jungle should be supplied with snake-bite kits and should have been trained in their use.

Some jungle rivers may contain additional dangers such as the crocodile or cayman or along the Amazon the piranha. Some large cats may still be encountered but will normally not attack humans without provocation. Often large jungle beasts of burden such as buffalo or elephant will be more dangerous if encountered without their handlers.

Still another danger is poisonous vegetation. The best defence against poisons such as ivy, oak, and sumac, among others, is good education in avoidance during jungle training.

Hygiene is important in the jungle to prevent disease. Operators should also have had their full battery of immunisations before deployment. Care must be taken in obtaining water in the jungle to avoid waterborne diseases. During the rainy season, rainwater may be used, but if it is falling from the jungle canopy, then fifteen to thirty minutes should be allowed for impurities to be washed off. All drinking water should be purified. Care must be taken, too, when crossing rivers in the jungle to keep the body fully clothed and bathing or swimming in jungle rivers should be avoided. Bacteria and fungi are common in the jungle and cleanliness, which is not always easy on operations, is the best defence against them. Operators in the jungle usually learn that it is better not to wear underwear, since it dries more slowly than outer clothing and often chafes the skin. Special care must be taken with the feet to keep them dry and powdered with foot powder. Spare pairs of socks are very important, too, to avoid problems caused by continuously wet feet.

The combination of high temperatures, high humidity, poor air circulation, and physical exertion require that operators in the jungle are alert for signs of dehydration, heat exhaustion, heat cramps, and heatstroke. Plenty of drinking water along with extra salt on food or salt tablets can help prevent heat maladies.

Local tribesmen in the jungle can be excellent allies to special operations forces or can be used by the enemy as trackers to locate them. Most special operations units are well trained in winning the trust of native populations, but some basic rules must be remembered:

- respect their privacy and personal property
- observe local customs and taboos
- do not enter a home without permission
- do not pick fruit, kill animals, or cut trees without permission
- treat the local population as friends

Frequently, jungle tribesmen feel dispossessed by a central government so operators who treat them well may gain loyal allies who are excellent sources of local intelligence.

Fortunately, food is normally abundant in the jungle if an operator has been trained to recognise edible fruits and vegetables and to trap or snare game. Shelter is important, especially in the rainy season, and should be built on high ground, away from swamps and dry river beds. Camps should be built well away from trails, game tracks, or villages. A great deal of intelligence can be gleaned in the jungle if the operator has been trained in tracking. Typical tracking points relevant to different environments include:

Savanna
- in high grass, grass which has been pushed down will not spring back for several days
- grass that is tramped down will point in the direction of movement
- grass that is pressed down will show a contrast in colour with the surrounding undergrowth
- when the grass is wet with dew, missing dew will show where a person or animal has passed
- boots may leave mud or soil on the grass

- if new vegetation is showing through a track it is old
- in very short grass, a boot will damage the grass near the ground and a footprint may be left

Rocky ground

- small stones or rocks may be rolled over or moved aside; the soil may be disturbed showing a variation in colour; on wet soil stones which have been displaced will show a different colour on the underside
- brittle stone may chip when walked upon leaving a light patch where the stone was broken and chips may litter the ground
- stones on a soft surface are pressed into the ground when walked upon leaving a ridge or a hole
- a boot may scrape off some of the moss from a stone

Primary jungle

- leaves may be disturbed on the jungle floor, often showing a darker colour if wet
- dead leaves or dry twigs will break when walked upon
- in thick undergrowth, green leaves on bushes that have been pushed aside will show the underside of the leaf
- boot impressions may show on fallen and rotting trees
- logs on the side of the path may show passage marks
- roots running across a path may show scrapes or deposits
- broken spider's web across a path can indicate movement along a path

Secondary jungle

- broken branches and twigs and leaves knocked off bushes or trees may indicate passage
- branches bent and footprints may indicate the direction of travel
- tunnels cut or pushed through vegetation and broken spider's webs will remain visible
- pieces of clothing caught on thorns or branches will be an obvious sign

Rivers, streams, marshes, and swamps

Signs that someone has passed include:

- footprints along the bank or in shallow water
- mud stirred up and discolouring the water
- rocks splashed with water in a quiet running stream
- water on the ground where someone has moved out of a stream, etc.
- mud on grass or other vegetation near the edge of the water

A US Navy SEAL in Vietnam blends into the jungle while setting an ambush (USNA).

Observing animal behaviour can also give early warning of the presence of danger. Proper jungle clothing will include light, fast drying fatigues worn loosely for ventilation and jungle boots which are light and fast drying with ventilated insoles and cleated soles for traction. When sleeping it is very important to erect a mosquito net even when a shelter cannot be built. Because of the heat and humidity in the jungle acclimatisation is important, but the acclimatisation time may be shortened for troops who have undergone a rigorous system of exercise to reach peak condition.

Since jungle fighting usually takes place at close range, often in meeting engagements, fast-reaction shooting on jungle lane training areas should be practised prior to deployment. Immediate action drills must also be practised so that a team can react quickly to an ambush. Since many jungle operations will be launched to hunt for guerrillas, special operations troops must be equipped and prepared to stay in the jungle for extended periods while tracking the guerrillas. If acting as guerrillas themselves, the operators will launch attacks on targets of opportunity, then retreat into the jungle to avoid stronger enemy forces.

When moving through the jungle operators will almost certainly have to cross streams or rivers. If they are shallow enough they may be forded, but if possible a site should be chosen where there is:

- good concealment on both banks
- minimal large rocks in the river bed as submerged rocks can be very slippery
- shallow water or a sandbar in the middle so operators can rest or regain their footing
- low banks to enter and exit the water

The stream should be forded at an angle against the current. Operators should keep their feet wide apart and drag their legs rather than lifting them so the current does not throw them off balance. Using a stick or pole to probe in front of the operator will help find deep holes and maintain balance.

Deeper rivers or streams may be crossed using various types of raft or flotation devices. The one-rope or two-rope bridge may also be constructed for crossing. Techniques for constructing rope bridges and for using them have already been covered.

When operating in the jungle, ambushes and defence against ambushes will be important tactical considerations. When constructing an ambush position, it should be borne in mind that jungles offer excellent concealment, but it will be necessary to work at finding cover. Normally, fighting positions should not be constructed in swamps or other low areas as they do not offer good fields of fire and are too wet to allow digging to obtain cover. Fortunately, jungles abound with possible natural cover including trees, rocks, logs, and rubble. Some jungle trees are especially dense and can stop high-powered rifle rounds, but others such as palm are soft and will not normally stop bullets. Natural cover is better, too, as it blends with the surroundings making it hard for the enemy to spot the position. Any artificial cover should be camouflaged to blend with its surroundings, and maximum use should be made of natural depressions and fallen trees.

Comfort should be given some consideration in building ambush or fighting positions, especially if the operators will occupy them for any length of time. If a position is dug, it should provide for drainage during the rainy season. An elevated floor of saplings can be easily constructed to keep operators from having to stand in mud or water.

Fields of fire must be given careful consideration when building a fighting position. Anything blocking the field of fire should be cleared

Selous Scouts practise counter-ambush engagement techniques (David Scott-Donelin).

away, but care must be taken that the area still appears natural, and leaves natural concealment. Generally, the operator's eyes and weapon should be at ground level so that he is concealed and protected from enemy fire. If a bush or tree is in the field of fire, it should not be cut down, though if necessary branches may have to be removed to allow target engagement; any marks left from trimming should be covered with mud. The jungle canopy should make it easy to conceal a position from aerial observation, but camouflage nets or vines and branches can be used if required.

The jungle canopy can make use of many types of radio difficult so radio operators must be familiar with techniques for constructing impromptu antennae among the canopy. Care must also be taken to protect the radios in waterproof containers.

When fighting in the jungle, tactics must always be dictated by the thick foliage and rugged terrain which limit fields of fire and slow movement. Engagements will normally come quickly as the team walks into an ambush or encounters enemy troops. Since sounds do not carry well in the jungle, an enemy may be much closer than an operator realises. For this reason learning to read the noises jungle animals make or their sudden silence can be very useful in avoiding a surprise attack. Surprise is a critical element in jungle tactics since the side which initiates contact and quickly gains fire superiority will normally have a decisive advantage.

Selecting a route when moving through the jungle requires weighing tactical considerations against ease of movement. Normally, ridge lines are easier for movement and land navigation because they avoid streams and gullies. Care must be taken, however, that operators are not silhouetted against the skyline since vegetation will be lighter on ridge lines. Stream beds and gullies offer much better concealment but are heavily covered with vegetation and slow down travel considerably. Roads or trails should definitely be avoided as they offer little concealment and will be well travelled. Ambushes or booby traps are most likely to be set along trails as well. It is possible in some circumstances to move parallel to a trail or road if looking for the enemy, but great care must be taken. Whenever moving in the jungle, a team must be careful to provide point, flank, and rear security to guard against ambush.

If attacked, the team must go into a coordinated immediate-action drill which will usually entail operators within the kill zone immediately laying down heavy fire while moving out of it. Other team members will deliver supporting fire. It may be advisable to pop smoke grenades to cover movement away from the ambush. Team members will normally have established a rallying point where they will meet if separated during the action.

When on the attack or when carrying out reconnaissance missions, the jungle lends itself well to infiltration. To move clandestinely, it can be advantageous if troops do not wear boots with a distinctive tread pattern immediately identifiable as from a western source. Recon teams in the jungle should travel as light as possible and should not leave any litter behind. When moving uphill, small saplings should be avoided as the shaking of overhead branches can be seen or heard at quite a distance. As has already been mentioned trails should be avoided unless the team is monitoring them, in which case they can move parallel to them very carefully. Unlike many other types of terrain, night is not always the best time for movement in the jungle as it is very dark under the canopy. A team with good NVGs, however, should be able to move if care is taken.

When a team stops for sleep or extended rest, care must be taken to establish 360 degree security. If possible higher ground should be chosen, and Claymore mines may be placed to cover all approaches. The same jungle features which allow a special operations unit to infiltrate an area will also allow an enemy force to approach quite near without detection.

If it is necessary to evacuate a special operations team from the jungle

Special ops personnel must be prepared to operate in hostile territory for extended periods (Larry Dring).

rapidly by helicopter special extraction methods may be a needed. The STABO system, which has previously been discussed, has been in use with special operations units for decades for the simple reason that it works very well. When a helicopter cannot land, the STABO system may be used to extract personnel from a clearing. When a pickup is to be made, a helicopter can hover at up to 150 feet and drop the deployment bag or bags (up to three) via the suspension rope. The operator to be extracted dons the harness, then attaches the bridle's snaphooks to the V-rings on his harnesses. After checking his leg straps are secure, the operator gives a hand signal or radios the helicopter that he is ready for liftoff. The chopper then lifts him clear and with the operator suspended beneath flies to a point where he can be lowered to the ground. The helicopter can then land to pick him up.

The Palmer rig uses a 120-foot nylon rope and two twelve-foot nylon sling ropes. Once it is lowered, the operator uses one of the twelve-foot

The jungle penetrator is designed to be dropped through heavy tree cover or ridden down to extract personnel (USAF).

ropes to form a sling around his chest and the other to form a rappel seat. He can then be extracted.

The Maguire rig is fabricated of nylon webbing sewn to form a loop containing a D-ring. A smaller slip loop is designed to hold the operators wrist while he sits in the larger loop to be extracted. The wrist loop secures him from falling through the other loop.

The Jungle Operations Extraction System (JOES) was designed to allow an operator to construct an extraction rig quickly from twelve-foot utility ropes and snaplinks, which can be dropped with the extraction rope. Basically, the operator constructs a rappel harness and seat from the twelve-foot utility ropes, then hooks on to the extraction rope. The JOES system works well with two operators hooked up facing each other during the extraction.

Some helicopters, such as this USAF rescue helicopter, are equipped with a winch for extracting personnel from mountains or jungle without landing (USAF).

Note that some extraction helicopters may be equipped with a winch system which will allow them to wind in the cable and bring the operators on to the helicopter, but this will not always be the case. Some helicopters such as the USAF 'Jolly Green Giant' may also be equipped with a jungle penetrator, a heavy metal penetrator designed to fall through jungle canopy and with a fold-down seat so that an operator can be winched up through the jungle canopy, though care to protect the face and hands must be taken. Normally, when any of these extraction methods are necessary, the operators are willing to put up with the discomfort of dangling below the chopper since the option of staying where they are has usually been removed by an approaching enemy.

Chapter 7

Intelligence-Gathering

Special operations personnel are often assigned the task of 'Special Reconnaissance', a term which can cover an array of missions. Even with the most effective satellite imagery, some intelligence must still be gathered on the ground, normally clandestinely. On some missions, surveillance and/or target acquisition may require special operators to infiltrate, establish a hide, and stay in place for weeks. Note that target acquisition normally has the primary goal of 'fixing' the target for air strikes, artillery fire, or ground attack, but the secondary mission is to update information on known targets. This can include checking that mobile launchers or artillery pieces which may move among sites in a relatively small area are fixed at the current location.

Normally, special operations reconnaissance units will be out of range of friendly fire support and resupply which will require them to survive on what they can carry since moving about in an attempt to live off the land is likely to compromise their mission. Often, too, operators inserted on such missions will wear 'deniable' clothing and carry 'deniable' weapons. Special Reconnaissance missions may also be carried out to make contact with indigenous forces who may assist special operations forces in unconventional warfare.

Typical strategic reconnaissance missions may include:

- establishing contact with indigenous resistance organisations and assessment of their combat potential
- collecting strategic political, economic, psychological, or military information
- evaluating enemy order of battle, Nuclear, Biological, or Chemical (NBC) capabilities, location of high-value targets such as headquarters or WMDs, and evaluating popular support for the government

Many special ops units train for years for counter-terrorist duties. In this photo the SAS carries out an assault at Prince's Gate, London (22nd SAS).

- collecting technical military information
- carrying out target acquisition as well as surveillance of enemy troop concentrations, strategic weapons, supply depots, transport hubs, terrorist training facilities, and other targets of strategic importance
- locating and gathering intelligence on hostages, PoWs, or political prisoners and the facilities where they are held
- carrying out post-strike reconnaissance
- gathering meteorological, geographical, or hydrographic intelligence to support planned military operations

The number of teams assigned to a specific strategic reconnaissance mission will vary depending upon the complexity of the mission. Surveillance of a single site may be carried out by a single team, while operations such as 'Scud hunting' during the First Gulf War absorbed a number of US Special Forces and British SAS teams.

One of the most effective yet simplest special operations techniques for gathering intelligence is the establishment of an observation post (OP) in enemy territory. The SAS has effectively used OPs during operations in Northern Ireland, the Falklands, both wars in Iraq, Afghanistan, and Kosovo among other areas. A well-established post may be in place for weeks without discovery and generate valuable intelligence. At Newry in Northern Ireland, for example, the SAS established an OP for weeks on a small platform behind the clock in the town-hall tower. In other cases, OPs were established to watch arms caches in Northern Ireland and this often led to arrests or ambushes when IRA members came to collect the weapons.

In the bleak damp terrain of the Falklands, OPs were cold, cramped, and wet, yet members of the SAS and SBS manned them for days to observe Argentine troop movements. Once the hides were constructed, thick plastic was placed on the floor in an attempt to keep out the damp, but it was a constant battle against discomfort. During the daytime, operators could not move around, light fires to cook, or talk. Even at night only minimal movement could take place and any fire for heating a meal had to be well hidden. Dealing with body waste is always a problem in an OP. Usually, it is necessary to defecate and urinate into bags, different ones as the mixture of the two types of waste can cause the bags to explode spraying their contents around the hide.

The choice of the site for the OP is very critical and considerations will vary based on the area of operations. For example, US Special Forces Manual FM 31-20-5 sets forth the following general considerations in site selection using the acronym BLUES:

Blend in with the surrounding area; the site should look natural and not attract undue attention.

Low to the ground construction, preferably in a position which provides protection against small-arms and heavier weapons fire

Unexpected sites should be used; a site should be chosen where enemy forces will not expect operators to be concealed

Evacuation routes must be planned during site selection; a link up plan with other members of the unit should be in place

Silhouetting the site should be avoided by using the sides rather than the crests of hills; do not get into positions where an enemy sniper or observer can see a silhouette.

Special considerations may apply when selecting a site in certain terrain. The following section considers the main types of terrain.

Urban terrain

Owing to limited fields of view in urban areas, more OPs than normal will have to be established to cover an area. As in SAS operations in Northern Ireland and US and British operations in Baghdad and other Iraqi cities, mobile surveillance may be carried out using vehicles. Taxis and delivery vans or even bicycles may be used when operating in areas which are not controlled by enemy forces. Taxis have the advantage that it does not appear odd if the driver is talking on a radio. Urban hides can be constructed in abandoned buildings, water tanks, shrubbery, factory chimneys, attics of tall multi-storey buildings, etc. Normally, wooden buildings should be avoided because of increased danger of fire or collapse. In situations where support elements are available, hides may also be constructed to look like something else (e.g., on top of a building a hide can be constructed to look like an air-conditioning unit). Note that in areas where urban combat is taking place, buildings may not be a good choice for OPs as they may attract artillery or rocket fire. Basements or rubble piles might make a better choice for establishing an OP. It is also important to be aware of booby traps and unexploded ordnance when occupying buildings in an urban area which has suffered sustained building to building combat.

In urban areas, the risk of detection is increased because of the concentration of people as well as lighting. On the other hand, if those manning the OP have good language skills and have adopted clothing which blends with the local population, detection may be harder since strangers are not so obvious. In urban areas under the control of a repressive regime, buildings often have some type of resident informant for the security forces so great care will have to be taken if operating from the basement or attic of an occupied building. This will extend to limiting use of electricity or water so that consumption does not suddenly go up. It must be borne in mind as well when using communications equipment that local security forces may have relatively sophisticated electronic counter-measures in place and may be able to locate the OP.

Mountain and arctic terrain

Mountainous terrain offers advantages and disadvantages for establishing OPs. The fact that movement is difficult makes it harder to get into position, but it also makes it difficult for an enemy to approach, especially quickly. The up-and-down nature of mountainous areas may require more OPs because of the limited fields of observation; however, above the tree line or in areas with light vegetation, a well-established OP can allow a substantial field of view. Generally, the site for the OP will not be

Special ops personnel must learn to operate in civilian clothes in an urban environment where skills such as vehicle counter-ambush are very important.

Special operations units train in tactics such as bus assaults.

Facilities such as this tyre house enable special ops personnel to develop their close-quarters battle skills.

determined by the height of the mountain but by available cover and concealment as well as the field of view. It may be most advantageous to establish one site for day observation and another for night observation. This will eliminate the need for personnel who man the day position, which will usually be higher, from having to move lower for night observation, which would increase the likelihood of being discovered. In some cases, if the advantages of sending observers into valleys outweigh the possibility of compromise, teams may move downward. In some cases observing upward at night, so that enemy equipment is silhouetted against the sky, will help identify it. When using optical devices, the snow cover may affect depth perception and obscure ground features; hence, the use of amber filters is advisable. If spotting for artillery, it must be borne in mind that deep snow may make ground bursts hard to observe so observers may request that initial rounds be airburst or coloured smoke. If sound-enhancing equipment is used it will often be more effective in valleys, too, due to a funnelling effect.

The irregular terrain in mountains offers hiding places for observers, but the rocky ground will normally make it difficult to dig hides. On the positive side, the rocks may be arranged to create a hide but care must be taken that it does not look too artificial. It is important that it blends in with the surroundings. If undergrowth impedes the field of view a few branches can be trimmed back, though once again care must be taken not to create an artificial-looking opening. The presence of caves in mountainous areas will often make them tempting as a possible OP site; however, enemy observers will immediately notice caves. Additionally, they will frequently be used by shepherds or others who move through the area.

Siting an OP above the snow line or when snow is on the ground presents a new set of problems. A site should be chosen in a shaded area if possible since in moderate temperatures body heat will have a tendency to melt snow, creating a bare patch. This type of melting is normal around trees, however, so if the site is placed near a tree it will be less obvious. Another advantage of the melt from tree limbs is that it can be used as a source of fresh water without needing a heat source to melt snow. Sites facing away from the equator will normally be more shaded. Remember, this will be the north slope in the northern hemisphere and the south slope in the southern. Shadows around rock outcrops or trees will have the advantage of hiding trails leading to the OP. Daytime melting of snow and night-time refreezing also increases the chance of avalanche which is another reason why shaded slopes offer an advantage. Another consideration in inserting a team into snowy areas is whether the use of a helicopter, the rotor wash of which will obscure any footprints left by the special operations team, is practical. If the helicopter insertion can be made without attracting too much attention, it may be more desirable than leaving long trails which will allow a team to be tracked.

In arctic conditions, one of the special considerations is that during summer there will be long hours of daylight and during winter long hours of darkness. Additional detriments to observation and/or comfort include cold, snow, fog, ice, and sleet. Shelters must take wind breaks into account. Dense north woods, downwind slopes of elevated terrain, and depressions all offer usable wind breaks. Snow caves may also be built. Normally, snow, ice, frozen soil, and timber will be the available materials from which to construct a hide, though sheet plastic liners and other light construction aids may be carried by team members. Sites must be chosen both to provide shelter and to provide an observation post, as the team must be able to survive to gather intelligence.

Desert

Generally, desert terrain has little vegetation for concealment combined with high temperatures, little water, sand storms, dust, fog, and haze. This combination makes concealment and observation more difficult and makes the discomfort level in an OP even higher than usual. Because of the lack of landmarks in the desert, GPS will have to be used for locating the special operations unit and for transmitting information about the location of enemy forces being observed. Experience at operating in the desert is very important for units manning an OP in this environment so that they learn to report accurately what they see without being fooled by mirages. Normally, the best time for observing in the desert is the early morning when targets are less likely to be obscured by dust clouds. On the other hand, the wind during the day may blow aside camouflage used to cover an enemy position. Of course, operators must also be aware that their own positions can be revealed if care is not taken in constructing them. Observation in the desert is much easier with optical aids, both day and night versions, so plans must be made for an OP to be well equipped with these devices.

Normally, the desert OP will be buried in the sand because of the lack of other cover. Units such as the SAS Mobility Troops have a great deal of experience at building desert hides and have learned what is needed to aid in their construction. As a result, materials to reinforce the sides or to support sand overhead may have to be transported to the site. Local rocks and boulders may be used to construct part of the hide, but it may also be necessary to transport a substantial number of empty sand bags which can be filled at the site and used for reinforcement. Plastic sheeting will also be useful for lining the hide.

Traditionally, from the days of the Long-Range Desert Group during World War II until SAS and US Special Forces patrols during the Gulf War, intelligence-gathering in the desert has been best carried out by mobile teams in Land Rovers or other high-mobility vehicles. In some cases, though, the use of vehicles which can be camouflaged to allow operators to construct a fixed OP in a critical location works especially well. The use of vehicles allows the operators to carry materials easily to construct a desert hide, too.

Forest
The greatest problem with establishing an OP in heavy forest is establishing a good field of view. One of the first decisions which will have to be made is whether to establish a ground OP or one in the trees. Ground OPs are easy to camouflage as tree stumps, fallen trees, undergrowth, etc., and are effective for watching paths, roads, or fire lanes for traffic. If streams, slopes, ditches, or other obstacles are located between the OP site and the path being observed that is even better, as these obstacles will slow any possible attack on the OP and are likely to

cause anyone approaching at night to make noise.

If an OP is to be established in the trees, the trees chosen should not be distinctive in height or shape so as not to draw undue attention. Although operators will be well camouflaged in the upper tree growth, getting into position can be difficult. Special climbing equipment and equipment for staying in place comfortably for extended periods will be necessary as will cover positions to support the observer or observers if they have to climb down quickly if detected by the enemy. Fortunately, most people do not look more than a couple of feet above their heads unless something attracts their attention, especially if carrying a military pack which causes one to bend forward at the waist. However, an observer in a tree must be very careful of movement as it will cause branches and leaves to shake and, thus, draw attention. A couple of pieces of wood from which to construct a tree stand or one of the prefabricated stands designed for hunters will make a tree OP much more comfortable and will make inadvertent movement less likely.

The biggest advantage of a tree OP is that a much longer view will be possible when in a heavy growth forest. On the other hand, if growth is very heavy all that the observer may see is other tree tops. The choice of tree for an OP is, therefore, very important and may entail climbing several trees to determine the best location. In some cases a tree OP can be combined with sensors seeded along trails so that the operator knows in which direction to search.

Jungle or swamp

Even more than with OPs in the forest, those established in tropical areas may have visibility severely impeded, dense vegetation often reducing visibility to thirty metres or less. On the positive side, this same thick jungle will offer operators excellent concealment. Movement through thick vegetation will generally be quite slow, which means that escape routes should be carefully reconnoitred. When choosing the site for an OP, the high water-table in swamp and some jungles must be considered as it will preclude digging. Because of operations in Malaya and Borneo, the SAS became quite adept at building bashas above the ground, and this same technique might work for OPs, though it would be necessary to camouflage them. When choosing the site for an OP, attention must be given to drainage, waterproofing, and security against reptiles and insects. Normally, local materials along with ponchos will be used to construct the site. A floating platform constructed of branches and timber layered over cross-posts will distribute weight and keep the observer off of wet, muddy soil. Jungle or swamp OPs will be most comfortable if hammocks are used for sleeping as well as storage of equipment to keep it off of the ground. Whatever the terrain, sites selected for surveillance should

- have an adequate line of sight to the target, both visual and electronic, while granting security to the operators
- have as wide a field of view as possible with as little dead ground as possible
- not be in terrain which will draw the attention of enemy forces (e.g., on top of a rock face on a hill or near natural drift lines for snow, sand, etc.)
- have covered and concealed exit and entry points
- be downwind from the target or villages at enough distance that dogs or people will not detect the site by smell; it must be borne in mind that wind directions change at different times of day
- maintain a distance from the target that is determined by a combination of mission and team security
- have good overhead and side cover and concealment
- be designed so that immediate action drills to break contact can be carried out if necessary
- allow good communications between observers and their command element, security element, or other support
- of extreme importance, should *not* be obvious to the enemy

Sometimes multiple sites will be used to allow observation during day and night or to watch different targets. To prevent an ambush if one site is not being used it should be kept under observation. It is also critical that operators do not establish patterns or leave trails when moving between sites.

Although site construction for observation posts will be based to some extent on the materials available locally, there are certain precepts which will apply to all sites. For example, site construction should take place during darkness and the site should be occupied before sunrise. A very complex site may actually take more than one night to build, however, so occupation may not be possible until after the first night. The first priority in building a hide is the external features since the inside can be improved after operators occupy it. Everything used for the site must be removed or replaced so that there are no indications that the local terrain has been disturbed. Special operations units will normally have rehearsed building sites under conditions similar to those in the area of operations. Members of the Royal Marines Arctic and Mountain Warfare Cadre or SAS Mountain Troops, for example, will have built numerous hides in mountain or arctic terrain and, hence, will be able to work more quickly on actual deployments.

One decision which will have to be made is what type of observation site best suits the mission and terrain. The most commonly constructed types include:

- *Above ground* Normally this type of site will be constructed when swift construction is necessary, there are few local materials to aid in construction, or the terrain makes it difficult to construct other types of hides. The primary disadvantages are that this type of site is easily detected and offers very little protection against hostile fire.
- *Spider hole* This type of site is basically a dug-in fighting position or foxhole with an overhead cover. The spider-hole will normally only be large enough to allow its occupant to kneel or sit. Usually, multiple spider-holes will be dug in a line or circle, one for each operator. This allows mutual support, better all around observation, and enhanced security.
- *Scrape* This is usually a temporary site, often for occupation at night using night-vision equipment. An existing depression will be enlarged to that one man can take up a position, probably prone. Overhead concealment will usually be provided by a poncho or camouflage net. Before vacating a scrape, the operator will usually try to obscure the fact he has been there.
- *Tent-type* This is, in effect, a large spider-hole for occupation by more than one man. Branches, bamboo, fibreglass rods, parachute lines, or other materials may be used to create a frame to hold a camouflage cover overhead. A shelf may be dug to support the tripod of a camera or telescope, and a slight arch may be included in the cover to allow ease of movement. Care must be taken, however, that the hide does not attract attention.
- *Underground* This is the safest type of site for the observers, but it is also quite difficult to construct. With only shovels or entrenching tools available, an underground hide can normally only be built in loose soil, though it can be built in sand if materials are available to shore up the sides and for use as a roof. Underground sites may also be built in stay-behind positions if enough time is available. For example, during the Cold War, NATO special operations personnel had access to propositioned stay-behind sites in case the Warsaw Pact overran most of Europe.

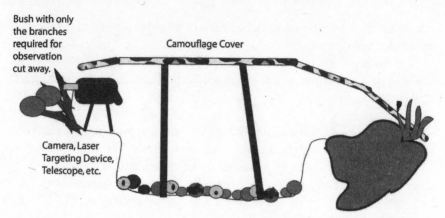

Figure 10   Tent-style observation site, camouflage should follow the natural line of the local terrain as much as possible; branches and twigs are placed on the floor to keep operators out of the mud. The sides can be lined with plastic if dampness or cold are a problem.

- *Bunker-type* This type of site requires even more time to construct than a standard underground site and lends itself even better to use as a stay-behind position. In some cases, special operations personnel may actually have developed kits for building bunker sites. Included will be tools needed to excavate and cut trees as well as plastic sheeting for waterproofing the roof, walls, and floor. Sandbags for reinforcing walls may be included as well.

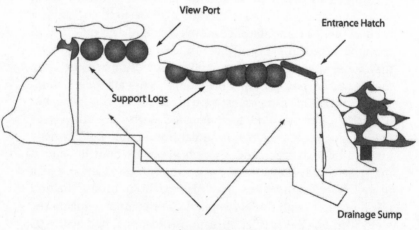

Figure 11   Underground observation site in snowy terrain.

- *Caves* Although caves offer an observation site which is already in existence, they also attract attention, are shown on maps, and may be used by locals for shelter or storage. Additionally, caves attract animals which may present health risks. Overall, the disadvantages of caves outweigh the advantages in most circumstances. Caves may, however, be useful for short-term observation (e.g., prior to an ambush).

Many special operations personnel learn some general construction principles for OPs which can be used in varied terrain and conditions. One of the first problems which must be addressed in constructing an OP site is removal of dirt. When soil is excavated it expands its volume. In drier climates, the soil below the surface tends to be a different colour; hence, when removed it must be camouflaged so it will not immediately indicate to an observer that digging has been taking place. By excavating prior to the point when early morning dew develops, the camouflaging process will be aided. Leaving the excess soil where the sun can dry it will also help in camouflaging it and may eliminate the need for any additional attempts at camouflaging it.

When it is necessary to camouflage removed soil, the following steps will normally aid the process:

- Lay out plastic sheeting, a poncho, or some other type of ground cloth.
- Place the topsoil, with vegetation if possible, to one side of the sheeting; bear in mind that topsoil only extends a few inches below the surface.
- Remove the remaining soil necessary to construct the hide, but keep it separate from the topsoil.
- Fill sandbags with the loose soil removed from the hole to create reinforcement for the sides of the site.
- Any excess soil remaining can be used to fill ruts, ditches, etc., nearby. If there are not depressions nearby, spread the excess soil lightly on the surface away from the hide. Do not put soil in streams or creeks as it may wash downstream and draw attention.
- Once overhead cover for the hide is constructed using logs or planks and it has been waterproofed with sheeting, replace the topsoil over it and add vegetation, leaves, and other materials scattered around the area to help camouflage the site.
- Fold up the sheeting which had been used to contain topsoil, then check the vegetation under it to make sure that it has not

matted from the weight. If it has, rake over it with a branch to make it look as natural as possible
- Periodically, check the vegetation and soil around the site to make sure that it looks natural and touch it up if necessary.

Taking care with vegetation around an OP can help retain natural camouflage. One simple task which will help keep vegetation alive is to water it during the site construction, especially if is has been displaced then replaced. When initially removing topsoil, it is important to save as much grass as possible. It can be removed in clumps by using an entrenching tool to cut around them in a circular pattern, then prying the roots and soil up from the bottom. When these divots (or turfs), which will usually run three to five inches in diameter, are replaced, the pattern should look as natural as possible. Shaking grass slightly to loosen the roots will help in the replanting as will a little water poured on the grass.

Larger plants are also important. Plants or bushes are an aid to camouflage but just as importantly they impede foot traffic around or over the site. Using plants on top of the hide may prove difficult, however, as they may die or fall over since the soil on top of the site will normally be too shallow.

Deadfall limbs or branches can also restrict movement near the site and grant camouflage, but in many of the areas where OPs may be established, deadfall is used for heating or cooking by the locals and, hence, will likely attract gatherers close to the OP. If deadfall is used as a combination of camouflage and cover from small arms, usually it should be reinforced with dirt.

As has already been mentioned, support for the sides of a hide is important for both safety and camouflage. Many sites will require side shoring to prevent cave-ins. Many field-expedient types of shoring can be used including local timber, branches, or deadfall. Light items carried in the pack such as plastic sheeting or ponchos will also work. Generally, however, the most effective shoring is sandbags. Not only can an operator carry a substantial number of empty bags in his kit, but they can conform to almost any shape necessary for shoring. Normally, special operations units will practise constructing hides to determine how many sandbags will be necessary for a typical site in the type of terrain likely to be encountered in the operational area. Then, they will carry this number plus ten per cent to allow for contingencies. Local freshly cut green timber can be used to cross brace sandbagged walls or prefabricated PVC pipe or conduit may be used as well if the unit is inserted by helicopter or using an all terrain vehicle.

As part of preplanning, many special operations teams develop prefabricated kits containing materials needed to construct an OP. The entire kit will not normally be taken on operations, but it can act as a stockpile from which to draw items for specific missions. Among the items likely to be included are:

- PVC pipe, various types of connectors for the pipe, and PVC cement; this combination allows the forming of various shapes to suit the terrain and size of the hide
- parachute suspension line, which can be used to form an interwoven frame for overhead cover when PVC is too bulky to carry
- sandbags
- various types of tape, cord, and rope
- plastic zip-lock bags
- half-metre plywood squares which can be used to construct overhead cover, platforms in tree OPs, ground insulation on ice or snow; these can be painted to match the terrain in which they will be employed
- heavy-gauge plastic sheeting
- tools including shovels, hack saws, hammers, small bow saws, axes, etc.
- plastic or aluminum tent stakes
- canvas and camouflage netting
- plastic buckets with formaldehyde
- mirrors or periscopes

Once an OP is built and occupied, then the primary task of intelligence-gathering by observing can begin. To enhance this mission, special operators normally receive training in effective observation techniques. During daylight, observers will first make a quick, overall search of their entire field of view looking for any anomalies including unnatural colours, silhouettes, or movement. Normally, the observer will first check the area directly in front of his position then scan outward. If the field of view is wide enough it may be best to divide it into subsectors and cover each in detail, usually alternating the search from right to left and left to right overlapping the previous subsector. For night observation, one of the most important steps for the operator is letting his eyes become accustomed to the darkness, a process which usually takes about thirty minutes in a darkened room or in the OP. When observing at night it is usually most effective to look slightly away from an object which will actually make it more visible. 'Scanning' an object by moving the eyes in short, irregular movements around it, pausing periodically for a few seconds will also help make it more visible.

Often, special operators will use compact video reconnaissance systems which may also be equipped with night-vision lenses. Not only may these video systems be used in the actual OP, but in areas with a high likelihood that an OP would be compromised they can be placed for remote operation up to ten kilometres from an OP. Images may than be sent via SATCOM to a higher command authority for action.

Among possible signs of enemy presence which should be observed are:

- *Sounds* Footsteps, sticks breaking, leaves rustling, men coughing or talking, vehicle or equipment sounds. Some of these indicators may be animal sounds so observers must learn to discriminate. Sounds are especially useful in determining the general direction in which an enemy may be located.
- *Dust or vehicle exhaust* Dust from moving infantry or vehicles as well as vehicle smoke will rise and is often visible at a distance.
- *Movement* While observing an area, movement will usually attract the eye, though the ability to determine whether leaves or limbs moving is the wind or an enemy sniper will take time to develop.
- *Positions* Especially areas where trained military personnel would establish positions including road junctions, hilltops, isolated buildings, and areas with cover and concealment. Remember, enemy special operations personnel will also be trained to avoid obvious positions.
- *Outlines or shadows* Soldiers, equipment, guns, or vehicles usually have distinctive outlines, but these may be concealed in shadows so check those areas carefully.
- *Shine or glare* Burning cigarettes, headlights, flashlights, even illuminated watch-dials can give away an enemy at night, while during the daytime reflected light or glare from smooth, polished surfaces such as windscreens, watch-crystals, or uncamouflaged skin can locate an enemy.
- *Contrasting colours* Even camouflage uniforms may contrast with background colours, as may uncamouflaged skin.

An important skill when carrying out clandestine observations is range estimation. Today, most special operators will have access to compact laser ranging devices to determine ranges quite accurately; however, the ability to do estimates remains important. Normally, 100-metre units of measure are used for estimates. Most Americans are used to visualising the size of a football field which is close to 100 metres in length. By attempting to calculate how many 100-metre lengths there are between two reference points a rough total can be established. Since many special operators now use rifles such as the M4 carbine equipped with the Trijicon ACOG optical sight, the ranging gradations on the sight may be used for estimation as well, though this will require a person or object of known size as a basis. Without an optical sight, the same method can be used if the observer knows how large a specific object appears at different distances. Operators can study a chart showing the sizes at varying ranges of objects likely to be encountered (e.g., Scud missile, standing man, truck, T-72 tank, etc.). With experience many operators will actually combine these two systems for range estimation. Flash and sound may also be used for range estimation if one can both see a weapon being fired and hear it. Based on the fact that sound travels at 300 metres a second, if an observer immediately starts counting (using the one thousand one, one thousand two, etc., method) when he sees the flash, smoke, or dust kicked up by a weapon being fired, then immediately stops when he hears the sound, a range estimate can be established by multiplying the number of seconds counted by 300 metres.

When reporting observations on enemy activity, US special operations forces are trained to use the acronym SALUTE as a reminder of critical information as follows:

Size	Generally, the number of soldiers, vehicles, tanks, missiles, aircraft, etc.
Activity	Basically, what the enemy is doing.
Location	Where the enemy is located using map coordinates or GPS.
Unit	If possible indicate the specific unit (e.g., 19th Guards Airborne Battalion) or, if it is not possible to identify it, try to indicate its equipment and type of uniform. Note indicators such as the wearing of NBC gear, which may indicate units prepared to launch chemical or other weapons.
Time	The time unit activity was noted should be reported, either in Zulu time (GMT in civilian terms) or the local time, whichever is applicable to the mission.
Equipment	Report all the types of equipment observed as the

information may be valuable when combined with other information available to intelligence analysts. If possible shoot digital photos which can be uploaded for analysis.

To give some idea of the types of information which can provide useful intelligence as it relates to specific terrain, more detail will be given on observation of an enemy force in an Arctic environment. First, special operations observers will want to answer two primary questions, how capable is the enemy of moving cross-country and how capable is the enemy of surviving and fighting for prolonged periods in extreme cold? To answer these two questions, operators will attempt to fill out a checklist which might contain the following questions:

- Does the enemy have skis and/or snowshoes?
- Do enemy personnel appear to be well-trained in using them?
- Does the enemy have specialised snow vehicles? What type?
- Does the enemy have specialised snow removal equipment? What type?
- Does the enemy have artillery? What type (SP or towed)?
- Does he have ski-equipped artillery or heavy machine-guns?
- How is the enemy moving equipment? Are there sleds or specialised transport?
- Does the enemy have heated shelters? What type and how many personnel do they hold?
- Are the shelters easily transportable without vehicles?
- Are improvised shelters being used?
- Does the enemy have winter clothing? Does it appear to be effective? Are there indications it is designed for specialised ski troops?
- What types of weapons does the enemy have? Do they appear to be effective in extreme cold? Are the heavier infantry weapons readily transported with the infantry?
- Does the enemy have aircraft – fixed-wing or rotor – available for transport and fire support? If so, what type?
- What logistical support does the enemy have?
- Are the troops airmobile?

When observing enemy troops during summer in northern areas, operators will also want to determine if the enemy has cross-country vehicles which can operate in marshy terrain, if he has boats, and if he has engineers with bridging equipment.

If special operations forces are more mobile in northern climates, they can watch for the following indicators of enemy troops in the area:

- signs of former encampments/bivouacs including packed snow, emergency shelters, remains of fires, trail networks, trash, freshly cut wood, etc.
- tracks in the snow left by men on skis or snowshoes, tracked vehicles, helicopters, aircraft using skis, air-cushion vehicles, snowmobiles, sleds, wheeled vehicles
- improvements to winter trails
- presence of winter landing fields
- ice bridges
- ice fog
- smoke
- manmade or mechanical sounds
- hot spots on IR sensors

Estimates of the number of an enemy in the area during cold weather operations may be obtained by observing the size and configuration of bivouacs, the size and number of tents in a bivouac area, the number of hot spots on IR sensors, and the number of trails in a given area. Similar checklists can be developed to fit other areas of operation and other enemies.

To aid in determining targets based on special operations intelligence, operators normally fill out checklists or reports using a rating scale between 1 and 10 to quantify various factors. For example, in determining the accessibility of the target a 9 or 10 would identify a target that was easily accessible and could be attacked with standoff weapons; a 7 to 8 rating would indicate a target inside a perimeter defence but not inside a building; a 5 to 6 would indicate inside a building but on a ground floor; a 3 to 4 would indicate inside a building but on the second floor or in the basement; and a 1 to 2 would indicate not accessible or accessible with extreme difficulty. Another factor considered is the recuperability of the target with a rating of 8 to 10 indicating that repair or substitution would take a month or more, with the scale running down to 1 to 2 which indicates same-day repair or replacement. Vulnerability is also rated with a target vulnerable to long-range laser target-designation, small-arms fire, or explosives charges of 2.2 kilos or less being an 8 to 10. Vulnerability to medium anti-armour weapons, explosive charges of between 4.5 and 13.6 kilos, or carefully placed smaller charges would rate a 5 to 6. Various other factors will be rated as well, including the effect destruction of the target will have on enemy capabilities and how easy it is to recognise in various light and weather conditions. By analysing this combination of factors special operations troops can determine whether a target is vulnerable to an attack with their own resources or whether they need to call in an air strike or artillery.

Although the use of observation posts to gather timely intelligence is an invaluable special operations mission, in many cases the targets assigned to special operations units are mobile, as were the Scud missile-launchers in the First Gulf War. Such targets move often and are dispersed to make them more survivable on the modern battlefield. In some cases, because of redundancy built into modern weapons systems, multiple attacks will be necessary to knock out the target.

Although mobile special operations units using fast, high-mobility vehicles can sometimes track mobile targets, it is often more effective to 'trap' the targets by identifying the most high-value mobile targets, anticipating their movements, and determining where to place special operations teams to create a network of traps for these targets. In some cases, special operations teams may attack targets of opportunity, but more often they will locate the targets and then call in airpower or artillery. Special operations personnel frequently study sophisticated enemy weapons systems so that they will better understand how to disrupt them by attacking the most critical components. For example, destroying missile-launchers will normally be more desirable than just destroying a missile, though both would be viewed as targets of opportunity. Part of the intelligence aspect of targeting these enemy systems will be determining where the key components of a weapons system are likely to be and when it will contribute most to the overall battle plan to disrupt these systems. At their most effective, special operations forces will provide their command and control element with a menu of high-value targets which they have located and which can be attacked as the assets are available or when it most contributes to the overall mission.

In some cases, mobile special operations units will be used to gather what is sometimes termed 'engineer intelligence' which can supplement information gleaned from aerial reconnaissance or satellite photos. Such information will be especially useful when special operations units are operating ahead of advancing conventional units or carrying out reconnaissance operations prior to the insertion of heavier units. They may gather information which relates to any or all of the following technical areas:

- *Roads* Their ability to support armour, likelihood of being washed out during a monsoon, etc.
- *Bridges, fords, and ferries* Of particular interest will be those which can act as secondary crossing points if primary bridges are destroyed. The ability of bridges to support various types of load will also be evaluated.
- *Buildings* Those which may be occupied by enemy personnel, high-value civilians (e.g., chemical warfare scientists, nuclear scientists), or which may be useful as HQs, field hospitals, etc.
- *Obstacles to troop movement* This can include natural obstacles as well as demolitions planted by the enemy.
- *Terrain* Forests, swamps, information on drainage, which ground can support mechanised forces, etc.
- *Underground features* Tunnels and caves; any underground bunkers or improved tunnels or caves should be described in as much detail as possible.
- *Materials useful to combat engineers* Quarries, stockpiles of steel beams, lumber, cement, or explosives, etc.
- *Engineering equipment* Bulldozers, sawmills, machine shops, etc.
- *Analysis of map accuracy* Military maps are frequently outdated or flawed even with the sophisticated technology available today. Reconnaissance troops can gain some idea of the accuracy of the maps troops will be using and possibly correct major errors. GPS will most likely be used to check correct locations of important landmarks.
- *Possible barriers to movement or fortified positions* Operators can determine positions likely to be used by the enemy as strongpoints as well as those likely to be useful to friendly forces during an invasion. Natural barriers which will impede mechanised movement such as deep crevasses or cliffs should be noted.
- *Rivers and streams* Width, depth, types of banks, crossing sites, navigability, pollution which might preclude use as drinking water. In winter the presence of ice floes which might impede crossings should be noted, as should likelihood of flooding during any anticipated operations.
- *Possible bivouac areas* Entrances, type of soil, availability of cover and concealment, etc.
- *Petroleum storage and equipment* In the case of Middle Eastern or other oil-producing countries, oil fields, refineries, etc., should be identified.

- *Utilities* Water, sewage, electricity, and gas facilities should be identified so they can be spared if possible and so they can be quickly put back into service after fighting in the area. Capture of utilities intact may be important to future civil affairs operations.
- *Ports* Teams should evaluate the docks, cargo-handling capacity, warehouses, transpiration to and from the port, and defences including mines and underwater obstacles.
- *Nuclear, Biological, and Chemical (NBC) warfare facilities* Trained operators should attempt to not only identify locations but also determine whether the facilities are in full production and ready to deploy weapons.

In a few cases, special operations teams will be sent in to carry out very specific intelligence surveys which require substantial specialised training. For example, prior to the commitment of large numbers of US troops a Field Epidemiological Survey Team (FEST) unit comprising Special Forces and epidemiologists from Walter Reed Medical Center was sent into Southeast Asia to plan for possible medical problems. Teams might also be sent in to determine whether or not WMDs had been used or were being produced in an area. Such teams would normally incorporate specialists or would require specialised training for team members in use of equipment and analysis or results. In some cases where normal communications intercept methods are not applicable, special operations units might be sent into an area to gather signals intelligence. This might require tapping landlines or even placing listening devices inside enemy facilities.

Since in the US Army, at least, civil affairs units normally work in conjunction with Special Forces, much of this intelligence as it relates to infrastructure will be useful post military operations to help stabilise an area.

Special operations forces may establish OPs or may track enemy weapons systems, both of which can provide timely tactical and, possibly, strategic intelligence, but often their most valuable intelligence will come from their local contacts with indigenous forces or local tribesmen. Indigenous allies can be especially useful to special operations personnel in gathering intelligence on enemy infiltration routes through jungles or mountain passes. By developing strong ties with local tribes that often do not like terrorist groups, guerrillas, or repressive government forces which operate in their area, a wealth of intelligence can be gained. The 'indigs' will often act as trackers or will help special operations personnel position their OPs. They can also act as an early warning system for special operations OPs, letting the operators know if the enemy is in the area.

Special operations forces working with indigenous tribesmen can act on intelligence by carrying out raids or acting as blocking forces against infiltrators, or they can use the indigenous troops to form a blocking force to catch the enemy retreating from an attack by airpower or conventional forces. USAF CCTs or equivalent special operators can work with indigenous troops to call in air strikes based on intelligence they have gained or as in the case of the Northern Alliance in Afghanistan to coordinate air support for irregulars.

Special operations forces may be called upon to carry out post-strike reconnaissance to assess the effectiveness of an attack either by friendly forces or enemy forces. Generally, post-strike reconnaissance should be carried out by satellite or aerial reconnaissance if possible to avoid endangering special operations forces on the ground. Certainly, special operations units should be used sparingly or enemy forces will expect them after a strike and set ambushes. As a result, only when the data is of absolute strategic importance should special operations be inserted for post-strike reconnaissance. Since, in some cases, the special operators will immediately call in a subsequent strike if the first one was unsuccessful, it is important to determine the minimum safe distance from which the reconnaissance may be carried out both to avoid detection by enemy forces and to avoid danger during a follow up attack.

If special operators do carry out a post-strike reconnaissance, they will usually attempt to determine the following:

- What weapon was used?
- What did the strike actually hit, including the point of impact, damage in that area, and collateral damage?
- Was the intended target affected in the desired manner (i.e., destroyed or disabled)?
- If the target was partially destroyed or disabled, what was the percentage of damage, and how far from the intended point of impact did the ordnance impact?
- Which specific part or parts of the target were hit or missed?
- How accurate was the pre-strike analysis and intelligence? If it was inaccurate, how far was it off?
- As a result of the strike, is the target still active and to what extent?
- Are there forces near the target carrying out rescue and recovery operations and are they employing any specialised recovery equipment or procedures (e.g., wearing decontamination suits)?

Another combined intelligence and direct-action role which special operators can perform in conjunction with local allies is location and rescue of downed airmen. In some cases, local tribesmen will have seen the aircraft go down and arrived on site ahead of enemy forces to rescue survivors. They may also be able to help special operations personnel locate the crash site or the point where airmen touched down after ejecting. Special operators can then call for rescue helicopters and help secure the area for extraction.

Naval special operations personnel are often used to establish OPs near the water or to carry out other intelligence missions which lend themselves to infiltration from the sea. US Navy SEALs define their intelligence mission as gathering information related to terrain, weather, or the enemy. Beach reconnaissance missions remain one of the most important carried out by naval special warfare personnel.

On counter-terrorist missions or missions to interdict enemy ship movements, naval special warfare personnel may also be used to gather intelligence about the following details which relate to raids against shipping:

- size of the ship, its type, its description; photos of salient features should be taken; including information about the hull, superstructure, etc.
- ship's specification including its range, speed, and engine types
- country of registration
- height of deck from the waterline and any ropes, ladders, etc., that will help with boarding
- hatches that are normally open
- nearness to dock or other ships, and normal activity on dock or ships at different times
- what type of activity normally takes place on deck at different times, including guard positions and changing times; note how guards are armed and whether military or paramilitary
- overall evaluation of difficulty of approach and scaling
- lighting on deck and lights pointed at the water; presence of security cameras or other intruder systems
- normal noise level on deck and whether generators and engines are normally running
- location of bridge and/or radio room
- small boats tied up to the ship
- whether there is a helicopter and/or helicopter pad

Naval special warfare personnel may also be charged with gathering intelligence for an assault on a harbour or dock as access to a larger installation or as part of a ship assault. If so the following information will prove useful:

- design of the dock
- materials from which it is constructed
- height from the waterline (at high or low tide if relevant)
- aids in climbing such as ladders, ropes, etc.; also whether pilings lend themselves well to scaling; whether they are covered in marine growth and, hence, slick
- noise and light level on the dock at different times
- telecommunications facilities
- bulk water supplies
- health services
- government administration and service offices
- security patrols and type as well as military personnel assigned; other pedestrian or vehicular traffic
- proximity of powerboats, fuel docks, maintenance facilities, or other buildings
- harbour patrol boats and schedule
- cover in the area including for sniper and/or cover team

Prior to a beach or shoreline assault, naval special warfare personnel may also carry out intelligence operations in addition to hydrographic reconnaissance. Information gathering may include:

- the type of objective
- the nature of the shoreline including sand, rocks, cliffs, and dunes, as well as the shape of the beach, straight, concave, or convex
- information about tides, waves, and currents, including information about high and low tides
- contour of the ocean bottom and if there are any manmade obstacles including mines, nets, etc.
- composition of the foreshore (the portion of the shore that lies between the extreme low water line and the upper limit of normal waves) noting silt, mud, gravel, boulders, rock, coral, or any combination of these; the gradient of the foreshore should also be determined as a ratio of water depth to horizontal distance
- marine life and growth

- proximity of roads, dwellings, or other buildings
- normal light and noise level
- beach patrols
- distances from the waterline to the objective and to cover or concealment
- escape routes either overland or out to sea
- suggested locations for assault teams, cover teams, snatch teams, etc.

While carrying out a beach survey, two swimmers will be assigned for every twenty-five metres of the beach to be recced. Depths are recorded starting at the point where the depth is about six-and-a-half metres and from there to the water's edge. As depth decreases, bottom samples are taken about every one-and-a-half to two metres or so (i.e., at five metres, three-and-a-half metres, etc.) During beach recces, combat swimmers must remain ready to go into immediate action drills should they be discovered. Normally, they submit a written report accompanied by detailed sketches, overlays, photographs, and samples from the bottom offshore and the beach.

Closely related to intelligence operations by special operations personnel are psychological operations (psy ops). US Special Operations Manual FM31-20 defines psychological operations as:

'... planned operations to convey selected information and indicators to foreign audiences to influence their emotions, motives, objective reasoning, and ultimately the behavior of foreign governments, organizations, groups, and individuals. The purpose of PSYOP is to induce or reinforce foreign attitudes and behaviors favorable to the originator's objectives.'

Among the uses of psychological operations are the following:

- To demoralise enemy troops and civilians by emphasising mistreatment of minority groups or repressive measures undertaken by the government. When used to improve morale of allies, psychological operations can emphasise victories or positive accomplishments.
- To reduce combat efficiency by stressing the personnel losses among enemy troops or civilians or pointing out economic losses.

- To encourage enemy troops, terrorists, or guerrillas to defect through surrender incentives such as dropping leaflets which they can turn in when surrendering. Convincing them that they face death and destruction if they continue fighting may also aid surrender, desertion, or unwillingness to take offensive action. Another ploy which has proven useful is convincing troops that they should return home to protect their families.
- To deceive enemy civilians, troops, or leaders with false information, especially that which can cause dissension among the leadership. Implications that members of the ruling party are corrupt or aiding an enemy can be effective as can leaked information about supposed alliances with sworn enemies (e.g., that an Islamic state is about to sign a treaty with Israel).
- On a positive side psychological operations can be used to establish national unity through emphasising common goals and attempting to educate tribal societies about loyalty to a nation.
- Positive psychological operations may also be used to keep the population informed about governmental programmes and successes. During SAS operations in Oman, transistor radios were supplied to tribesmen at low prices so that they could receive positive information about the government and its programmes to help the tribesmen.
- A psychological operations campaign can be used to redirect the interests of a population away from a negative and towards a positive. For example, in an oil-rich state, to direct attention away from Western workers, a programme can be launched showing the economic benefits to every citizen from oil revenues.
- By creating a positive or negative image of leaders their status can be enhanced or lowered in the minds of their supporters.
- In some cases, psy ops will be used to present truthful information to a population used to receiving false information from news sources. This will develop an audience for broadcasts, websites, etc., which the audience perceives as truthful.

Psychological operations personnel may work with special operations personnel but may not actually be trained special operators. However, special operations units may do the initial intelligence-gathering to help determine what the mission for psychological operations will be. Likewise, psychological operations support units will help prepare special operators for their missions. This may include briefing them on factors which can influence the reliability of indigenous peoples with whom they may have to work. Warnings about groups who might betray the operators because of fear of reprisals from the government can be invaluable in keeping special operations teams alive. Because special operations units often cannot accomplish their missions without the assistance of the local population, the importance of psy ops becomes magnified, especially in insurgencies or counter-insurgencies.

Another important function psychological operations can provide to support special operations is educating special operators to consider that any of their acts which affect a local population can have an impact on their mission – positive or negative. Four factors which should be given special considerations are:

- impact of noncombatant casualties
- permanent presence of hostile security forces in a populated area
- relationship between hostile security forces and the civilian population
- effects of combat operations on morale of friendly and hostile forces

The special operations personnel can provide useful information to psy ops planners as well. For example, as they work with indigenous guerrilla forces or tribal allies, special forces can determine what groups can be effectively targeted by psychological operations. This may entail identifying the various societies present in a given country. Once there is a basic understanding of the society, groups which can assist the special operations mission can be identified for psychological operations. Disaffected and underrepresented minorities (or in some cases, majorities) can be targeted and psy operations can assist in recruiting them as allies. Once target groups are determined, then the methods to best influence them must be chosen based on their access to communications, their value systems, and other factors.

Since special operators can normally function closer to enemy forces than other personnel, they can often employ psy ops targeted specifically at enemy military forces, especially since their ability to operate in their 'safe' areas is already demoralising. Normally, psy ops targeting enemy military forces will try to make them feel:

- isolated
- improperly supported

- doubtful of the outcome of the conflict, especially in their ability to win
- distrustful of each other, especially of their political and military leaders
- doubtful of the morality of their cause

Because they can operate across borders, special operations troops may also help in disseminating 'black propaganda' which claims to come from a source other than its true one. By infiltrating enemy territory, for example, and broadcasting as what is purportedly a government radio station black propaganda can be given credibility. Often, black propaganda will be attributed to dissidents within the enemy country, a tactic which can be effective both in influencing the population and in generating paranoia within a repressive regime. If written by skilled psy ops personnel, messages can even be given the same style as typical enemy propaganda, thus increasing its credibility. Because of the difficulty in establishing its source and its clandestine nature, black propaganda is difficult to refute with counter-propaganda. Some black propaganda can demoralise an enemy without even using actual propaganda. Spreading counterfeit currency, ration cards, or identity cards can erode confidence in the government. Even more direct action such as planting ammunition rigged to explode in the weapon, then spreading the word that quality control at government arms plants is bad, can make troops far less willing to engage in combat. Or planting inflatable boats along coastlines or leaving parachutes in trees along with supplies which appear to be for a guerrilla force can destabilise local government authority.

If specialist psychological operations personnel are not deployed to an area of operations, special operations teams may be charged with preparing psychological operations contingency plans, which they might have to implement in cooperation with psychological operations teams. These plans will normally deal with possible events such as intervention by another power or the sudden cessation of hostilities. Usually included in contingency plans will be information about:

- realistic objectives based on the additional variables
- an analysis of the likely effects of the possible events on the population, the military situation, and the political situation
- sources of information used in preparing the assessment/plan and sources which will be useful if it has to be implemented
- clarification of the target group within the population
- themes which will be used to achieve the desired objectives

- media to be employed to reach the target group

Particularly, if intervention by a hostile power is feared or if a hostile power is supporting insurgents in an area where special operations personnel are giving military assistance to a friendly government, psy ops can be used to convince the hostile power that it is not in their best interest to continue their support; raids by special operators to destroy weapons or supplies intended for the insurgents or other operations which 'punish' the hostile power can aid in this objective. Using psy ops it is possible to persuade them that the insurgents will fail or that the advantages of supporting the current government outweigh opposing it; this objective will often employ a carrot-and-stick approach.

When special operations troops help disseminate propaganda to aid in fighting a counter-insurgency, among themes pursued might be the following:

- making the population aware of civic action or other programmes designed to help the targeted population and pointing out the successes of these programmes
- persuading the local population that supports the guerrillas that their goals can be achieved through the political process
- showing the futility of guerrilla warfare including its cost in lives and effects on the economy of the country
- pointing out that the guerrilla movement is not really a national liberation movement but is under the control of an exterior power which has an agenda counter to the best interests of the citizens
- pointing out that guerrilla leaders are bandits more interested in their own aggrandisement and enrichment than in the people
- influencing international opinion against countries supporting the guerrillas
- explaining the necessity and reasons for population and resource controls to deprive the guerrillas of support
- exposing fallacies in the insurgents' ideology

However, those involved in psy ops must normally be aware of certain taboos against propaganda which may be counter-productive. Generally, the following themes will be avoided in dealing with other cultures:

- boasting or sneering
- ridiculing or degrading of the target audience as citizens or

soldiers (however, there may be a few exceptions as with an army perceived as oppressive and divorced from the people)
- name-calling
- using obscenities, oaths, or foul language
- using pornography
- invoking religious issues, though pointing out that Marxist states are atheistic has proven effective
- making promises which cannot be kept
- delivering ultimatums without the capability to enforce them
- demanding unconditional surrender except in circumstances where it can be enforced and total and visible defeat of the enemy is desired
- sabotaging of communications media, though in some circumstances this is necessary to eliminate the source of enemy propaganda or terrorist communication
- urging assassination of leaders
- using deception
- using divisive techniques targeting tribal or family groups instead of the government or military
- dispensing untruths, though partial truths may be used for security reasons to protect sources or as part of a destabilisation campaign

Although these taboos will normally be observed as has been mentioned, with some of them circumstances may arise when using these methods has more advantages than disadvantages. For the most part, however, they offer sound guidelines for special operations and psy ops personnel who must work with the local population and who do not want to alienate them unnecessarily.

Special operations troops may also be charged with assisting friendly troops and building awareness of psy ops. For example, special operations units with personnel who speak local languages may often help liaison in dealing with former guerrillas or terrorists who come over as part of an amnesty programme. In cases such as the Selous Scouts in Rhodesia, some of these former guerrillas/terrorists may be formed into hunter/killer groups against their former allies.

Psy ops in support of special operations may require a great deal of care to ensure that the implementation of a psy ops programme does not hinder the overall mission. For example, if special operations troops are assisting a host nation in fighting a counter-insurgency, then any initiatives should appear to come from the host nation rather than the nation giving the assistance. Care should be taken so that it does not appear that the special operations forces are taking civic action or otherwise assisting the population because the host government is unwilling to do so. In the case of special operations units carrying out guerrilla warfare and raising irregulars, they will often have to take advantage of opportunities for psychological warfare as they arise and be willing to think creatively in gaining propaganda benefit from their operations and contacts. When special forces units are assisting in civil affairs projects, these can often be used by psy operations personnel to paint the government in a positive light but how the activities are 'spun' is very important. Finally, special operators may take part in counter-propaganda missions against enemy agents by eliminating the agents, jamming their broadcasts, shutting down sources of print propaganda, helping create counter-propaganda, and gaining allies among religious, professional, and political groups influential among the population.

US Special Forces and the SAS among other special operations units engage in civic action programmes to win the hearts and minds of the local population during counter-insurgency operations. Psy ops can enhance civic action programmes by doing the following:

- making the population aware of the plans for economic, political, and social improvements
- re-educating the public by offering them truthful news emphasising the positive aspects of civic action programmes
- addressing the reasons for disenchantment among the population and countering guerrilla or terrorist propaganda
- working on building the morale of the population
- stressing the cooperation between counter-insurgency or counter-terrorist forces and the population

In the US Army, Psychological Operations and Civil Affairs fall under the Special Operations Command which makes combining psychological operations with various types of special operations much smoother.

Chapter 8

Survival, Evasion, Resistance, Escape

S ince special operations troops frequently operate in enemy-
controlled territory, they must assume that at some point their
mission may become compromised, forcing them to escape and
evade (E&E). At some point, too, the special operator may find himself
separated from other team members and far from friendly support. As a
result, he may have to survive off the land until he can be extracted or can
reach friendly or allied troops. The experiences of the Bravo Two Zero
patrol of the SAS during the Gulf War offer a perfect example of why
special operations troops must be capable of taking decisive action if their
mission is compromised.

Special operations troops are normally trained to approach survival
with an acronym based on the word SURVIVAL:

Size up the situation
Undue haste makes waste
Remember where you are
Vanquish fear and panic
Improvise
Value living
Act like the natives
Learn basic survival skills

In other words, in sizing up the situation, the operator will get to a safe
place and evaluate his own situation (e.g., asking himself, is he injured,
what does he have with him which will help him to survive, etc.). He will
then attempt to determine where he is and how he can reach safety.
Finally, he will evaluate enemy capabilities and threat. He must bear in
mind that he may know where the enemy is, but the enemy does not
necessarily know where he is.

In avoiding undue haste, the operator must take care not to move so fast that he makes mistakes or exposes himself to the enemy. It may be better, too, to rest for a while or to wait for night. In remembering where he is, the operator must not make mistakes that draw attention to himself such as smoking, leaving debris or garbage behind, or forgetting possible natural dangers such as snakes or dangerous terrain. The operator may not be able to vanquish fear completely, but he must be able to use it. Fear can cause the operator to be cautious and can give him a shot of adrenaline which will allow him to keep going. Though he must ponder his situation, he should not dwell upon his loneliness or isolation lest he panic or go into a funk. By planning the steps necessary to survive and implementing them, he can focus on what he is doing to change his situation.

Survival

Improvisation is always a key element of survival. Training can teach operators to find food, water, medicine, and shelter in seemingly hostile environments. A safety pin can hold together torn clothes, but it can also act as a fish hook or part of a snare to capture food. By continuing to value living, the operator will fight to survive against the elements, the enemy, and his own doubts. One reason military survival training is so tough is the need to teach operators to reach down within themselves to keep going. Keeping the focus on getting out alive is important. Acting like the natives will allow an operator to use the local environment to his advantage and, in some cases, to blend with a local population by donning local garments, though he must bear in mind that as long as he remains in uniform, if captured, he has the status of enemy soldier. Finally, by learning basic survival skills before they are needed, the operator will be prepared when he finds himself deep in enemy-controlled territory or deep in the desert, jungle, or mountains.

One of the first steps in preparing for survival is developing a basic survival kit designed for the area of operations. Most special operators have a basic kit which they carry in their pockets or on their belt. It normally contains such basic items as a good folding knife (possibly a Swiss Army Knife or a multi-tool), fire-starter, water purification tablets, fish line for fishing and making snares, fish hooks and/or safety pins, needle and thread, and a compass. The items already listed will probably fit in a pocket in some type of waterproof pouch. If a belt pouch is used, additional items may include candles and waterproof matches, a folding E & E map, heavier cord, aspirin, wire for trip wires, clear plastic bags of different sizes for use in purifying water and making solar stills, salt tablets, surgical tubing (which can be used to create a slingshot, for drinking, and in making snares), a solar blanket, and tape. If it will fit, a compact GPS device should be included as well. Finally, additional items useful for survival can be carried in the rucksack including more rope, a ground-to-air survival radio, heavier duty knife, a poncho or Gore-Tex jacket, and changes of clothes. Some special operations units issue a .22 calibre suppressed pistol for silent killing, but it may also be used for silent hunting in a survival situation.

Although this manual can only give an overview of military survival techniques, I highly recommend 'Lofty' Wiseman's *Survive Anywhere Safely* as a detailed source of survival techniques. Special operators should have received training in the following survival skills:

- water procurement and purification
- field-expedient direction-finding and land navigation
- shelter construction (with special emphasis on areas of likely deployment)
- building fires
- making ropes from local materials
- signalling
- butchering, preparing, and smoking meat
- making impromptu tools or weapons (e.g., a spear)
- creating traps and snares
- fishing
- identification of edible plants and their proper preparation
- emergency first aid, including plants which may be used for medicinal purposes

Evasion

When isolated in a hostile area an operator or operators must first make decisions about their best way to avoid capture by the enemy. In some cases, as in a downed helicopter, the best recourse may be to stay put and wait for a rescue chopper to arrive. However, since enemy patrols may have shot down the helicopter or seen its crash, it may be necessary to move to another pickup site or to move away from the immediate area and hide until the enemy presence thins. If an operator is separated from other members of his unit, his first action should be to move to the last rallying point or to a prearranged rallying point chosen in case of separation. If rescue is unlikely, then the viability of reaching friendly forces must be considered and possible routes evaluated. Still another possibility is to reach guerrilla forces or others opposed to the local government and join them to fight as partisans until exfiltration is possible. Some US personnel did just this in the Philippines during World War II.

In forming the evasion plan, enemy activity in the area must be observed. If there is more than one operator who will be evading, then the decision must be made whether to travel separately or in small groups, though two or three is the maximum which is normally desirable. Stock must be taken of the distance that will have to be covered, the availability of food and water, and the best route. An alternative route should be chosen as well. Normally, movement should be at night, and the day should be used to rest, plan, and observe any enemy activity. Most special operators will have received at least some training in tracking and counter-tracking; these skills must be used to cover their tracks as much as possible. Roads and populated areas should be avoided as should abandoned dwellings, though, in harsh weather, an abandoned cabin might be the difference between life and death. If maps are used, they should not be marked as this might give an enemy information about escape and evasion routes or location of friendly forces. It may be necessary to use silent killing techniques to eliminate enemy personnel if there is no other way to get past them.

In some cases, special operators will have assistance in evading capture. There may be local guerrillas friendly to the operators or local dissidents who dislike the government. In some cases, evasion routes may already be established and operated by guerrillas. Operators may have been briefed on the availability of assistance in evading or may be briefed via radio when it becomes obvious they will have to evade. Normally, though, operators will take care not to compromise a local network unless given orders to contact them or be contacted by the guerrillas.

When operating in an area where many of the locals are not actually engaged in guerrilla warfare but do not like their government, 'blood chits' will often be issued which inform locals in their own languages that the bearer is friendly and that a reward will be given for his safe return to friendly hands. Some operators are also issued gold coins which can be used to bribe locals for food, shelter, transportation, or other assistance; however, showing this money might actually attract undue attention. When well-organised E & E networks are in place, they may be able to provide operators with false documents, clothing, guides, local currency, transportation, and information about enemy forces in the area. When contacting in-place E & E networks, care must be taken in approaching contacts that the operator does not compromise them or attract attention from security forces with the contact.

At all times when receiving assistance from local populations, however, the operator must remain alert to betrayal and have contingency plans for quickly moving out to carry on his evasion. When deployed on counter-insurgency operations, in fact, unless a tribe is known to be loyal to the government or to the special operations assistance forces, then any locals should be considered likely supportive of the insurgents or at least intimidated by them.

Many special operations units have an established 'evasion corridor' along which they are expected to move in evading capture. Often, there will have been predesignated recovery points along this corridor so that the operators know where they might expect to link up with friendly forces or expect exfiltration by helicopter, boat, etc. These recovery points are usually chosen based upon estimated travel time combined with terrain features which lend themselves to rescue operations. Prior to the mission, personnel usually fill out a form with personal information which can be used to verify that it is actually the operator asking for exfiltration rather than enemy troops who have captured his survival radio and are using it to set an ambush for rescuers.

If the operator is not rescued and must reach friendly troops on his own, then as he approaches friendly units, care should be taken to approach only in daylight and to observe them before approaching. Before approaching, it is normally best to call out first to make sure they realise that they are dealing with 'friendlies' rather than the enemy.

It may prove necessary to cross a heavily patrolled border. The operator should watch for electrified fences which may be indicated by the presence of dead animals or insulators. The possibility must be considered, as well, that the border is mined, covered by guard towers with snipers and searchlights, or patrolled by dogs. A plan to cross the border should be based on observing any patrols and their routines and should use night, bad weather, or distractions of the guards. The operator must be aware of any curfews which are in effect near the borders as checkpoints and patrols will likely be more intensive.

Although survival is discussed in conjunction with E & E it is important to remember that when attempting to escape and evade, little time will be available to carry out survival tasks such as trapping, gathering firewood – especially since a fire will give away the operator's position – or building shelter.

Resistance

Because special operations troops operate a good portion of the time in territory controlled by the enemy, often on sensitive missions, if captured they are likely to be interrogated extensively. As a result, special operations training normally includes segments on resisting interrogation and surviving as a prisoner of war. The basic rules which most special operations soldiers are expected to follow include:

- make every effort to escape and help others to escape
- do not accept special favours from the enemy
- do not give your word not to escape
- do nothing that will harm a fellow prisoner
- give no information except name, rank, serial number, and date of birth
- do not answer questions other than those related to name, rank, serial number, and date of birth

Although all special operators will try to adhere to these basic rules or similar ones, it must be assumed that they will be tortured for information. As a result, operators are normally trained to resist torture and interrogation for a given amount of time, usually based upon how long it will take to extract other teams about which they may have knowledge, change call signs, and otherwise take measures so that any information possessed by the operator cannot compromise ongoing operations. Once the operator has held out as long as possible, it is usually considered acceptable for him to give the interrogators small pieces of information which will alleviate the torture or harsh treatment.

During interrogation, it may not be advisable for a special operator to admit to knowing the local language as this may be advantageous for gaining information and if he escapes. He should not admit to being Special Forces, either. When confined with anyone other than members of his own team, the operator should be careful of informants. While being interrogated, the operator should be polite and respectful but unco-operative. It is advisable not to look the interrogator directly in the eyes as this might convey information by the operator's expression when asked certain questions. It is better to look at the interrogator's forehead or between the eyes. The operator should not volunteer false statements as this might give the interrogator an opening to elicit real information.

In many cases, captors will attempt to indoctrinate the operator in their philosophy. Repetition, harassment, and humiliation may all be used as part of the process. The interrogators will especially be looking for 'weak links' whom they can indoctrinate, then use against others. Special operators should have been trained to understand the Stockholm Syndrome and avoid psychologically identifying with their captors thus eroding their will to escape.

While in captivity, it is necessary to retain self-discipline and confidence in one's will to survive. Morale must be kept up and fear controlled. Health care is important. Anything edible should be eaten to keep up the operator's strength, and he should practice as much personal hygiene as possible. Planning an escape will not only prepare the operator if the opportunity to flee arises, but it will help maintain his will to survive. Towards the possibly of escape, anything which might be useful for an escape should be hoarded.

Escape

Normally, the best time to escape captivity is shortly after capture as the enemy will be in some disarray. Friendly fire or air strikes may cause some confusion, thus providing a chance for escape. The first guards assigned are unlikely to be as well trained at handling prisoners as prison guards and will not have guard towers, dogs, etc. Some of the first guards assigned may well be walking wounded who will be distracted by their own condition. An operator will know something about the area where he was captured and may even have additional equipment cached nearby. Shortly after capture, too, the operator will normally be stronger than after mistreatment and starvation. There is no set method of escape that is best in these circumstances but the general rule of escaping early and when the enemy is distracted virtually always applies.

As part of their escape, evasion, and interrogation training, operators will normally meet with former PoWs and those who have successfully escaped from enemy captivity. Not only will these discussions help them learn techniques but they also gives them graphic examples of others who have survived the experience. This training will include techniques for escaping from PoW camps based on prior experience.

Tunnelling has been a traditional escape method but is normally based on the assumption that personnel will be held in barrack-style camps. Tunnelling is usually less viable for those held in bamboo cages or stone cells, though it is not impossible. In fact, to exit the camp, the operator may have to go over a wall or wire fence or through the wall or wire. In some cases, it has actually proven easier to walk out the gate disguised as a civilian worker. Since special operations personnel are usually captured operating in jungle, desert, or mountains, once they do escape from captivity, they are likely to have to survive in a harsh environment while attempting to reach a border or friendly troops. However, if held in a city, then they may need to obtain stolen or forged ID cards and passes in order to travel. At least some special operations troops will have received training in forgery and may know how to fabricate official-looking stamps from shoe soles, linoleum, wooden blocks, or even potatoes.

Although training will often include incarceration in a simulated PoW camp and the operator will learn various escape techniques, the most important aids to escape will be observation and flexibility. By watching the routine of the camp, biding his time until an opportunity arises, being prepared to capitalise on that opportunity, then carrying out an escape if the opportunity is presented, the operator has some chance of success. Special operations training in general toughens operators mentally and physically. Additional training in surviving captivity and escaping give them a certain confidence in their ability to take advantage of any opportunity to escape or, at least, not to give up hope.

Suggested Reading

Bennett, Richard M. *Elite Forces: The World's Most Formidable Secret Armies*. London, Virgin, 2003.

Camsell, Don. *Black Water: A Life in the SBS*. London, Virgin, 2000.

Clancy, Tom. *Special Forces*. NY, Berkley Books, 2001.

Couch, Dick. *The Finishing School: Earning the Navy SEAL Trident*. New York, Crown, 2004.

Couch, Dick. *The Warrior Elite: The Forging of SEAL Class 228*. New York, Crown, 2001.

Crawford, Steve. *The SAS Encyclopedia*. Miami, FL, Lewis International, 1998.

Davies, Barry. *SAS: Shadow Warriors of the 21st Century*. Miami, FL, Lewis International, 2002.

Desert Operations (FM 90-3) Washington, DC, HQ, Dept of the Army. August, 1993.

The Jumpmaster (TC57-1) Washington, DC, HQ, Dept of the Army. September, 1979.

Jungle Operations (FM 90-5) Washington, DC, HQ, Dept of the Army. August, 1982.

Long-Range Surveillance Unit Operations (FM 7-93) Washington, DC, HQ, Dept of the Army. October, 1995.

Micheletti, Eric. *Special Forces War on Terrorism in Afghanistan*. Paris, Histoire and Collections, 2003.

Northern Operations (FM 31-71) Washington, DC, HQ, Dept. of the Army. June, 1971.

Pathfinder Operations (FM 57-38) Washington, DC, HQ, Dept. of the Army. April, 1993.

Pushies, Fred J. *Weapons of Delta Force*. St. Paul, MN, MBI, 2002.

Pushies, Fred J. et. al. *US Counter-Terrorist Forces*. St. Paul, MN, MBI, 2002.

Ranger Handbook (SH 21-76) Ft. Benning, GA, US Army Infantry School, 2000.

Ryan, Mike. *The Encyclopedia of the World's Special Forces*. New York, Barnes & Noble, 2003.

Ryan, Mike. *Secret Operations of the SAS*. St. Paul, MN, MBI, 2003.

Sasser, Charles W. *Encyclopedia of the Navy SEALs*. New York, Checkmark, 2002.

Special Forces Free-Fall Parachuting (FM 31-19) Ft. Bragg, NC, US Army Institute for Military Assistance. August, 1977.

Special Forces Operational Techniques (FM 31-20) Washington, DC, HQ, Dept of the Army. December, 1965.

Survival (FM 21-76) Washington, DC, HQ, Dept of the Army. October, 1970.

Survival, Evasion, and Escape (FM21-76) Washington, DC, HQ, Dept. of the Army. March, 1969.

Thompson, Leroy. *The Bodyguard Manual*. London, Greenhill, 2003.

Thompson, Leroy. *The Counter-Insurgency Manual*. London, Greenhill, 2002.

Thompson, Leroy. *The Hostage Rescue Manual*. London, Greenhill, 2001.

Index